Pat Collins CM

Finding Faith

in troubled times

THE COLUMBA PRESS
DUBLIN

First edition, 1993, published by
THE COLUMBA PRESS
93 The Rise, Mount Merrion, Blackrock, Co Dublin

ISBN 1 85607 066 2

Cover by Bill Bolger
Origination by The Columba Press
Printed by Loader Jackson Printers, Arlesey

Nihil Obstat:
Thomas Norris DD
Imprimi Potest:
✠ Desmond
Archbishop of Dublin
25 November 1992

Contents

Dedicated to the memory of my parents
John and Babs Collins
Who by word and example, taught me how to be anchored in God

Introduction

Sometime before she died my mother told me that, as a young woman she had prayed that she would meet the right man to marry, someone who would take the things of God as seriously as she did herself. With that intention in mind, she even went to the penitential island of Lough Derg for a couple of days, to pray that God in his providence would enable her to meet the right person. Afterwards she felt that my late father, whom she referred to as her 'rock of Gibraltar,' had been sent to her by God. He was a man of deep, unpretentious faith, and like her, a daily mass goer. I was touched and amused to discover that during their honeymoon, my mum and dad had promised to pray together every day of their married lives. Indeed, shortly after my father's death in the mid seventies, my mother was able to tell me that they had fulfilled their promise. As she said herself, 'You must realise that your father and I were anchored in God.' When she herself died a few years ago, I had a look through her bedside cabinet. Among her many books I found a well worn copy of the New Testament, which was literally falling apart as a result of constant use. In was another indication that she, like my father, had been sustained throughout the years by her relationship with the Lord. It was this sense of the mysterious Other that was imbibed in different ways by my brothers, my sister and myself.

Since then, like many other cradle Catholics I have had to struggle to understand the Christian faith within the changing circumstances of the late twentieth century. As someone living in the Post Enlightenment era, of depth psychology, existentialism, relativity, quantum physics etc., I have tried to articulate the Christian vision for myself and for others, in in a way that is orthodox, credible and relevant. Over the years I have found that I have had to let go of some of the naive understandings of scripture, dogma and ethics that would have satisfied my parents. With St Paul I can say, 'When I was a child, I spoke like a child, I thought like a child, I reasoned like a child; when I became an adult, I put an end to childish ways' 1 Cor 13:11. Instead of weakening my faith, this process of painful maturation has strengthened it. As John Paul II has rightly observed, 'The critical spirit of science purifies religion of a magical conception of the world and of surviving superstitions and exacts a more and more personal and active adherence to the faith.'[1] In the following chapters, I want to share some reflections on different but interrelated facets of faith which in recent years have helped me, like my parents, to be anchored in God.

In retrospect I can see that the four themes that I have chosen to write about, have been influenced by scripture and the liturgy. For example, they are all present in Mk 16:15-19, where the risen Jesus says to the apostles, 'Go into the whole world and proclaim the good news to the whole of creation. The one who believes (Faith) and is baptized will be saved; but the one who does not believe will be condemned. And these signs will accompany those who believe: by using my name they will cast out demons (Exorcism); they will speak in new tongues; they will pick up snakes in their hands, and if they drink any deadly thing, it will not hurt them (Freedom from fear); they will lay their hands on the sick, and they will recover (Healing).'

The book begins with an exploration of the nature and implications of believing the good news mentioned by Mark, and which is referred to in the eucharistic prayer as the 'mystery of faith,' namely, that Christ's blood was 'shed … for all, for the forgiveness of sins.' I may say in passing, that some of the material in this section originally appeared in shorter form as a chapter entitled 'Faith and Ministry', in a book entitled *New Beginnings in Ministry*.[2] In section two, we go on to examine the whole question of anxiety. Mark says that God in his providence can protect those who believe in him from unforeseen dangers. This need is adverted to in the words 'protect us from all anxiety' which are said before holy communion.

As we know, evil is the source of untold suffering in the world, and as such it is one of the greatest barriers to relationship with God. Section three of the book goes on to ask whether we still need to believe that evil can be diabolical in nature. It will also explore how, in the words of the liturgy, we might be 'delivered from every evil', e.g. by casting out demons in the name of Jesus. In the fourth and final section, we will look at the way in which people can experience 'healing of mind and body', not, in this instance, through the laying on of hands, but by receiving Christ in the Eucharist. A shorter version of this section appeared as an article entitled, 'The Healing Power of the Eucharist', in the 1992 edition of Aquila.[3]

The Church has been afflicted in many ways since the Second Vatican Council. It is my belief that we are about to experience the affliction of secular society. In the coming years it is quite possible that we will have to endure a time of economic and social upheaval which will lead to all kinds of unrest and violence. We cannot predict what the outcome of such a crisis might be. While it will not be caused by the Lord – it is in fact the logical outcome of our Godless attitudes, values and preoccupations – the Almighty will use it for his purposes. Through painful events he will address these words to both lukewarm Christians and unbelievers alike, 'Seek the Lord while he may be found, call upon him while he is near; let the wicked forsake their way, and the unrighteous their thoughts; let them return to the Lord, that he may have mercy on them, and to our God, for he will abundantly pardon' Is 55:6-8. It is my belief that the Lord is urging us to repair the breached walls of our Christian lives by means of repentance and conversion.

When Nehemiah saw that the walls of Jerusalem had been breached, he urged the faithful to rebuild them. 'You see the trouble we are in,' he declared, 'how Jerusalem lies in ruins with its gates burned. Come, let us rebuild the walls of Jerusalem, so that we may no longer suffer disgrace' Neh 2:17. This image is a metaphor or image of the state of the Church in our day. I share the conviction of those who believe that the walls of our spiritual lives have been badly damaged by the pursuit of material things and what has been called an á la carte approach to morality and belief. This kind of moral relativism and doctrinal reductionism can leave the Church very vulnerable to the insidious incursions of evil. Unless Christian leaders warn people of the current dangers while summoning them to the all important task of renewal, the Lord will have reason to say, 'I sought for anyone among them who would repair the wall and stand in the breach before me on behalf of the land... but I found no one' Ezech 22:30. As Pope St Gregory the Great has explained, 'To go up into the breaches means to withstand the powers of this world and defend the flock by speaking out freely.' [4]

It is my hope that by speaking out freely in the following chapters I might help you to identify and to mend those breaches in your spiritual life where the winds of adversity blow, where the jackal of instinct cries, and where the enemy enters under the cloak of darkness. Francis Bacon has said, 'Some books are to be tasted, others to be swallowed, and some few to be chewed and digested: that is, some books are to be read only in parts; others to be read but not curiously; and some few to be read wholly, and with diligence and attention.'[5] It is my prayer that, despite their limitations, you will want to chew and digest, these reflections in a prayerful way. They will have served their purpose if they help your faith to develop in a way that is orthodox without being re-actionary, credible without being compromised, and relevant without being simplistic.

Finally, I want to express my gratitude to Angela Mc Anespie and Marie Fox D.C. for their encouragement, support and practical help throughout the writing of this book. I'd also like to thank the staff of All Hallows. Over the years I have been inspired by their unity of mind and heart, their dedication to mission and ministry, and their academic competence and liveliness. They are a living embodiment of Newman's ideal of an integrated approach to Christian truth and wisdom. Its motto could be 'All truth, no matter by whom it is uttered, comes from the Holy Spirit.'[6]

All Saints Day, Nov 1st 1992
The 150th Anniversary of
the foundation of All Hallows College

PART ONE

Living the Mystery of Faith

'The spirituality of the future will not be supported or at any rate will be much less supported by a sociologically Christian homogeneity of its situation; it will have to live much more clearly than hitherto out of a solitary, immediate experience of God and his Spirit in the individual'

(Karl Rahner, *The Practice of Faith*, p 21.)

CHAPTER 1

The Faith that Saves

A number of years ago I heard a parable which made quite an impression on me. In its naive way it described what could be referred to as life's crucifixion points of powerlessness. They are the moments of vulnerability when we consciously encounter our desperate need for God. As such they are the birthplaces of faith.

A blackbird and a crow lived in the same tree. The blackbird used to sing sweetly and effortlessly from dawn to dusk. As for the crow, no matter how hard he tried, he could only squawk. He thought to himself, 'If I observe the blackbird closely, I may discover the secret of her singing.' After a while he did notice that she had a different diet to his. He changed his, but to no avail. He continued to squawk. Then he noted that the blackbird had a different timetable to his. So he trained himself to imitate her pattern of waking and sleeping. It made no difference however. He still continued to squawk. When he told a couple of passing jackdaws about his dilemma, they informed him about a school for birds some miles away. 'Why not go there for a year or two,' they said, 'and take a course in music. When you qualify, you may be able to sing like a blackbird.' The crow heeded their advice. For two arduous years he learned about the theory and practice of music. When he returned to his tree, the blackbird was still there singing as sweetly as ever. The crow flew to the highest branch, took in a deep breath, proudly opened his beak, and launched into a squawk! The moral of the story? No matter how hard he tries, a crow will never be able to sing like a blackbird.

It seems to me that the same is true in our lives. In spite of our intelligence, knowledge, experience, skills, efforts and good intentions, there are many things we cannot change. As contingent creatures for example, we will never be the adequate explanation of our own existence. As sinners we can neither earn nor merit the saving grace of God. Nor can we live out our lives in accordance with the Lord's will. Speaking on behalf of of us all, St Paul said, 'I do not do the good I want. But the evil I do not want is what I do...Wretched person that I am, who will save me from this body of death?' Rm 7:19;24. Like the hapless crow in the parable, we have to come to terms with such crucifixion points of powerlessness. Time, and time again, in the midst of our daily struggles we have to acknowledge that all will be lost, if God does not sustain us. That is where faith comes in. One could say that it is the quality or power which enables the things we desire in our powerlessness to finally become, by the grace of God, the things we experience.

Faith in Contemporary Thought

Like a many sided diamond, the subject of faith has been examined in recent years from various overlapping points of view. In a well known description, Paul Tillich[1] has referred to religious faith as the state of being ultimately concerned by what is truly and solely ultimate, namely, the ineffable mystery of God. Maurice Blondel's[2] analysis of human action led him to the conclusion that the will which produces action cannot satisfy itself, because its deepest desire is never fulfilled by any finite good. So although a person might not seem to have faith at the conscious level of conceptual expression, the seed and the potential for such faith might well be implicit in the person's dedicated and purposeful activities. Gregory Baum[3] and Peter Berger[4] have gone a step further by examining the 'depth experiences' such as friendship, conscience and humour which can lead people to affirm the meaning of reality and thereby the God who undergirds its intelligibility. Martin Buber[5] a Jewish writer has explored the distinction between interpersonal and propositional notions of faith. Cantwell Smith[6] has furthered this approach by meticulously examining the evolving relationship between interpersonal faith and different forms of belief, from an historical point of view. In recent years, rather than focusing on the content of faith, James Fowler[7] has focused on faith as a universal activity. It can mature through six developmental stages, each of which is characterised by increasing degrees of cognitive complexity and comprehensiveness, which may or may not have a religious content.

Bernard Lonergan[8] who described faith as 'knowledge born of love,' maintains that such a disposition has to be incarnated anew in our culture which is in a process of fundamental change. It is moving from 'classical' to 'historical' forms of consciousness, i.e. from a static world view which stresses the importance of objective authority to a dynamic one that stresses the importance of subjective experience. The current crisis of faith, he says, is a misnomer. In fact it is essentially a cultural crisis which requires a reformulation of 'the faith' in contemporary categories of thought. Otherwise it will appear to be increasingly irrelevant in a fast changing world. Lonergan's observation reminds me of a story about an immigrant boy in New York city. When asked if his family had found a home yet, he answered, 'We have a home already, we just have to find a house to put it in.' Through their faith in Christ, present day Christians have a spiritual home. But they have yet to find a contemporary intellectual framework in which to house it, one that is adapted to the quantum age in which we live.[9]

In recent years process philosophers and theologians such as Whitehead, Hartshorne, Ogden, Cobb, Pittenger, de Chardin, Griffin etc., have made brave but ultimately unsatisfactory attempts to formulate a new overarching theory which could embrace the best insights of modern science and theology. In a recent book,[10] which itself has been influenced by process thinking, Fritjof Capra, a well known scientist, sketches a list of characteristics for 'new-paradigm thinking' in science. He does this in the context of a dialogue with Benedictine theologians, David Steindl-Rast and Thomas Matus. They, for their part, have suggested that the theology of the future will probably be influenced by the following five characteristics which are analogous to the ones already outlined by Capra:

1. There will be a shift from God as a revealer of truth to reality as God's self-revelation.
2. There will be a shift from revelation as timeless truth to revelation as historical manifestation.
3. There will be a shift from theology as an objective science to theology as a process of knowing.
4. There will be a shift from building e.g. through principles, laws etc., to networking, e.g. stressing the inter-

connections between theological statements, as metaphors of knowledge.
5. There will be a shift from theological statements to divine mysteries.

Time will tell whether, these signposts will prove to be correct. I suspect that they do contain more than intimations of the way in which faith will be housed in the future.

In an exceptionally helpful article Avery Dulles[11] has maintained that faith includes three elements: a firm conviction regarding what is supremely important together with dedication or commitment to that which one believes in, and trustful reliance on the power and goodness of whoever or whatever one is committed to. The three components of faith are thus conviction, commitment and trust. On the basis of this description Dulles has suggested that currently there are three models of faith operating in people's lives.

Firstly, there is the intellectualist approach, which can take two forms, the illuminationist and propositional. The former sees faith in Platonic terms as infused wisdom of a contemplative kind. The latter sees faith as a firm assent to the truths which the Church authoritatively teaches in the name of God. By and large theologians such as Anselm and Thomas Aquinas adopted this approach and it informs programmatic spiritualities e.g. the Ignatian Exercises would exemplify the illuminist approach and *The Way* of Josemaria Escriva de Balaguer the propositional.

The fiducial approach emphasises the fact that faith is a form of trust in the God of the word and the word of God. It stresses the importance of personal relationship with the Lord. God is more a saviour than the revealer of truth. The fiducial notion of faith tends to turn in expectation and hope toward the future. People like Luther, Wesley and St Thérèse of Lisieux adopted this approach and it informs contemporary forms of evangelical and charismatic spirituality.

The performative approach, sees faith as 'a liberating power that 'saves' life, giving it wholeness and efficacy, in the midst of bondage, estrangement and guilt.' People like Sts Vincent de Paul and Louise de Marillac adopted this approach and it informs the liberation theology and spirituality currently emanating from the South American Church.

While being aware of the importance of these interrelated points of view, I will not be focusing on them in this section. Rather I will reflect, with the help of scripture, on saving, trusting and charismatic types of faith. They have become increasingly important to me in recent years. I am including the third form, for three main reasons. Firstly, it seems to me that when Jesus referred to faith, he often had the charismatic kind in mind. Secondly, the faith to do deeds of power such as healings and miracles is neglected in modern theology, exegesis and spirituality. Thirdly, I believe that this sort of faith has an important role to play in present day evangelization and ministry. Finally, we will take a brief look at faith when God seems to be silent and absent. In this chapter however, we begin our exploration by looking at the faith that saves.

Saving Faith

What is known as the theological virtue of justifying faith is the bedrock of the Christian life. As Jesus said before his Ascension, 'Whoever believes and is baptized will be saved' Mk 16:16. Like the apostles before him, Paul had discovered that, 'Faith comes by hearing the message ... and how can people hear without someone preaching to them' Rm 10:17;14. For example, when the jailer in a Philippian prison suspected that all his prisoners had escaped following an earthquake, he decided to commit suicide. As soon he realised this, St. Paul shouted, 'Don't harm yourself! We are all here.' Having brought them out, we are told that the jailer 'rushed and fell trembling before Paul and Silas.' Evidently, he had reached a decisive crucifixion point of powerlessness. Acutely aware of his urgent need, he at last found words to express what he had probably felt in a vague, inarticulate way, many times in the past. 'Men what must I do to be saved?' he cried out on his own behalf and on behalf of countless numbers of people down the ages.

Paul responded to this all important question, by giving a one line summary of the gospel. 'Believe in the Lord Jesus,' he said,' and you will be saved - you and your household' Acts 16:25-35. This reply echoed what he had written on other occasions., 'If you confess with your mouth, 'Jesus is Lord,' and believe in your heart that God raised him from the dead, you will be saved,' and again, 'Everyone who calls on the name of the Lord will be saved' Rm 10:10;13. Presumably Paul went on to expand on his succinct answer, by telling the jailer about the core truths of Christianity, which are sometimes referred to as the kerygma,[13] e.g. 1 Cor 15:3-8. Like the jailer and his household the Acts repeatedly attest that those who greeted the good news with faith were baptized immediately. By receiving the sacrament of initiation they were immersed, drenched, soaked and innundated in the saving grace of Christ the Lord.

The Foundations of Faith

Nowadays most people are baptized as infants. But it seems to me that many of us have failed to consciously appropriate the saving grace of the sacrament through personal faith in the foundational truths of the Christian religion i.e. the kerygma. In fact, as I have suggested elsewhere,[14] we are currently living through what could be called a kerygmatic crisis of head, heart and hands.

The kerygmatic crisis of the head refers to knowledge i.e. to do with intellectualist faith. Many Christians today are ignorant of the basic teachings of the scriptures, and their primary importance within the hierarchy of revealed truth. As a result, they fail to appreciate the fact that, for example, the divinity of Christ is of greater significance than the assumption of Mary or any moral teaching. As Pope John Paul II has said, 'It is less possible than ever today to stop at a Christian faith that is superficial or of a sociological type; times as you know, have changed...It is necessary to arrive at a clear and certain conviction of the truth of one's Christian faith, namely in the first place, the historicity and divinity of Christ and the mission of the Church willed and founded by him.'[15]

The kerygmatic crisis of the heart refers to awareness i.e. to do with fiducial faith. Even when they have a notional grasp of the good news, many Christians fail to experience the liberating power of God's unrestricted mercy and love in their personal lives. It is when we are drenched, soaked, and innundated in the Spirit of the risen Jesus, that these truths drop the vital eighteen inches from head to heart, thereby leading it 'into the truth about God.' Jn 16:13. It is this awareness that provides committed Christians with the desire and the power to live as true disciples of the Lord. As Karl Rahner wrote near the end of his life, 'The Christian of the future will be a mystic or he or she will not exist at all. If by mysticism we mean... a genuine experience of God emerging from the very heart of our existence.' He goes on to add, 'It is only in the light of an experience of God, which is the real basic phenomenon of spirituality, that theological indoctrination by scripture and the Church's teaching acquires its ultimate credibility and existential enforceability.' [16]

The kerygmatic crisis of the hands refers to action i.e. to do with performative faith. Is it any surprise that those who neither know nor experience the power of the kerygma in their lives, fail to witness to it in their words or actions. All too often they seem to live like those who have not been baptized. They appear to separate religion from life and to walk by sight and not by faith. St James posed a relevant question in this regard when he asked, 'what good is it, my brothers and sisters, if you say you have faith but do not have works?...faith by itself if it has no works is dead' Jm 2:14;17. Echoing these words Pope Paul VI commented on May 19th. 1975, 'We would say only this: today you either *live* (my italics) your faith with devotion, depth, vigour and joy, or that faith dies out.'

Law without Evangelization

Because the Catholic Church sometimes wrongly presumes that all its members are evangelized, it places the full yoke of discipleship on their shoulders e.g. with regard to sexual and marital morality. If such people have not come into a personal relationship with Christ or experienced his extraordinary mercy and love, they may have the desire to carry the yoke that is placed on them by the Church, but they will not have the power to do so. For example, a baptized couple will find that even if they neither attend Mass or pray, they won't have much difficulty being married in church. As man and wife however, they will be prevented from using contraceptives, or getting an abortion. If in time the marriage fails, they will find that it is impossible to get a divorce and almost impossible to get an annulment or to be married again in church.

To people who have not been evangelized, the Christian ethic, is not a 'yoke that is easy and a burden that is light,' (cf Mt 11:30). Instead of being a way of liberation it can become a way of oppression. Perhaps Jesus would say to the Church of our day, 'You tie up heavy loads and put them on people's shoulders, but are not willing to lift a finger to move them' Mt 23:23;4. Is it any wonder that many baptized Christians, turn their back on the Church because they associate it with bad rather than good news. What is needed is evangelization, a kerygmatic proclamation which is aimed at head, heart and hands, by people who have already experienced its liberating power in their own personal lives.

Catholic and Protestant views of Salvation

In the light of the last point, I suppose it is not surprising to find that committed evangelical Protestants sincerely believe that in spite of being baptized many, if not most Catholics are not saved. In their view, R.C's are not born again because they fail to make a conscious decision to give their lives to Jesus Christ, by accepting him as their personal Lord and Saviour. There is a classic description of what they mean in the life of John Wesley. Following his ordination as an Anglican priest he went to the American Colonies. In spite of the fact that he was a conscientious Christian he got into trouble because of an improper relationship with a woman. Shortly before his return to England he met a Moravian pastor who challenged him in a profound way. Wesley recounted their conversation in his Journal 7 Feb. 1736. He said, 'My brother, I must first ask you one or two questions. Have you the witness within yourself? Does the Spirit of God bear witness with your Spirit that you are a child of God?' I was surprised and knew not what to answer. He observed it and asked, 'Do you know Jesus Christ?' I paused and said, 'I know he is the Saviour of the world.' 'True', replied he, 'But do you know that he has saved you?' I answered, 'I hope he has died to save me.' He only added, 'Do you know yourself?' I said, 'I do.' But I fear they were vain words.'

17

The Protestant Experience

Some time after his return to England, John Wesley's desire for a deeper relationship with God was answered. Again he described what happened in his Journal on 24 May 1738. 'In the evening I went unwittingly to a society in Aldersgate Street, where one was reading Luther's preface to the Epistle to the Romans. About a quarter before nine, when he was describing the change which God works in the heart through faith in Christ, I felt my heart strangely warmed. I felt I did trust in Christ, Christ alone, for salvation. And an assurance was given me that he had taken away my sins, even mine and saved me from the law of sin and death.' In our own day Billy Graham, the renowned Protestant evangelist, makes a Weslian-type appeal to his listeners and readers alike, 'If you have never accepted Christ into your life, I invite you to do it right now before another minute passes. Simply tell God you know you are a sinner, and you are sorry for your sins. Tell Him you believe Jesus Christ died for you, and that you want to give your life to him right now, to follow him as Lord the rest of your life. 'For God so loved the world, that he gave His only begotten Son, that whoever believes in him should not perish, but have eternal life' Jn 3:16.'[17] Graham then goes on to assure the born again that all their sins are forgiven and that they are new creations in Christ. Over the years I have been moved, edified and inspired by Protestant men and women who have testified to this type of salvation experience. That said, I have come to see that in spite of its obvious merits, this challenging point of view can have a number of limitations.

Firstly, in my experience many evangelicals are inclined to talk about salvation in the past tense, as something they have already experienced in a definitive way. But surely it is something on-going. (cf 1 Cor 1:18) While it may have already begun, salvation will only come to fruition if the person being saved continues to cooperate with the grace of God. Secondly, some 'saved' Christians can have a problem admitting serious sins they may have committed after their salvation experience. This is so, because they seem to be so incompatible with the definitive grace they claim to have received. This can lead either to a certain blindness where wrongdoing is concerned, or in some cases to a morbid sense of defeat and despair. Thirdly, those who believe that they are already saved, sometimes suffer from an off-putting self-righteousness. They believe that a majority of mankind, including many of their fellow Christians, are on the path to perdition, no matter how good and sincere they might seem to be. Fourthly, those who stress the evangelical understanding of salvation are often quite poor at building upon that foundation stone. Instead of developing an elaborated spirituality which takes account of the purgative, illuminative and unitive stages of spiritual growth, they are inclined to keep going back to the milk of the foundational experience. (cf Heb 5:12) Fifthly, I have noticed that some evangelical Christians seem to overlook the material needs of the poor and to be surprisingly uncritical of the socio-political status quo. Jim Wallis a Protestant himself, has written a challenging and relevant critique of the political complacency of some evangelical Christians.[18] Lastly, because they seem to overlook the fact that their theological outlook is conditioned by things like historical circumstances and a rather literalist reading of Scripture they can fail to appreciate the Catholic experience of salvation.

The Catholic Point of View

The Council of Trent responded to the Protestant doctrine of Justification by faith alone, in the following three steps. Firstly, 'Adults are disposed to justification as follows ... by believing to be true what has been divinely revealed and promised especially that the sinner is justified by God's grace 'through the redemption which is in Christ Jesus' Rm 3:24. Secondly, 'when, understanding that they are sinners and turning from the fear of divine justice – which gives them a salutary shock – to the consideration of God's mercy, they are aroused to the confident hope that God will be favourable to them because of Christ.' Finally, 'when they begin to love God as the source of all justice and are thereby moved by a certain hatred and detestation for sin, that is, by the repentance that must be practised before baptism.'[19] In this statement the Council seemed to be talking about the kind of faith that leads to adult baptism. The bishops went on to say that the Protestant claim that one had to be inwardly certain of having been saved through faith was not correct. 'For just as no devout person should doubt God's mercy,' write the Council Fathers, 'so also, whoever considers his or her personal weakness and lack of disposition, may fear and tremble about whether he or she is in the state of grace, since no can know with a certitude of faith which cannot be subject to error, that he or she has obtained God's grace.'[20] The Church Fathers then went on teach about how it was important to cooperate with the grace of salvation by means of on-going good works, willing participation in Christ's sufferings etc.

While the Protestant approach might seem a bit strange to a majority of Catholics, the goodness, love and fidelity of a great many of them, provide ample evidence of the fact that they are indeed experiencing saving grace. By participating in a sacramental community this precious gift can be appropriated by means of an on-going process of osmosis and conversion. Having begun in baptism,[21] it often occurs in a real, but largely non-conceptual way e.g. by receiving the sacraments, forgiving hurts, accepting suffering in union with Christ, avoiding sin, showing concern for the less fortunate members of society etc. This explains why, although many devout Catholics fail to express their awareness of redemption, in terms of a dramatic conversion experience, and in a formula of words which would satisfy the expectations of evangelical Protestants, their experience is essentially the same as that of 'born-again' Christians.

However, we know that there are many 'cradle Catholics,' have been sacramentalised without being evangelized in either an explicit or implicit way. In Cardinal Newman's terms, their faith seems to be more notional than real. Lacking a conscious and committed sense of relationship with the triune God of the New Testament, it is not surprising that there are predictable effects to be seen in their everyday lives. While many people, like these, continue go to Mass on Sundays in a conformist sort of way, 'they honour God with their lips, while their hearts are far from him' Mt 15:8. Many others rarely spend time in prayer or appear in church, unless they have reason to attend a baptism, marriage or funeral. In either case, the ethical values and attitudes, of a large number of such practising and non practising Catholics, seem to be moulded by the world rather than the gospel (cf Rm 12:2). One would suspect that if they were put on trial for being

Christians, there wouldn't be sufficient evidence to find many of them guilty. So all things being equal, the dangers associated with sociological Catholicism are just as real as those which are sometimes associated with evangelical Protestantism.

That said, I suspect that Hans Kung's is correct when he makes the theological assertion that as far as justification is concerned the teaching of Tent and the Protestant reformers can be reconciled. In any case, from the point of view of the marketplace, experience has taught me that believing Catholics and Protestants have a lot to learn from each other and their respective experiences of saving grace. For example, in an age when programmatic spiritualities are being replaced by more personalist ones, Catholics would do well to augment their sacramental orientation by learning from their separated brothers and sisters. They could stress such things as the value of regular scripture reading, and the need for a deliberate personal commitment to Jesus as, 'the Way the Truth and the Life' Jn 14:6. For their part, 'born again' Protestants could learn from Catholics about growing in wisdom and grace by means of the purgative, illuminative and unitive stages of spiritual development. In any case we can evaluate our differing approaches by adopting the rule of discernment used by Jesus when he observed, 'By their fruit you will recognise them' Mt 7:16, and again, 'Not everyone who says to me, 'Lord, Lord,' will enter the kingdom of heaven, but only the one who does the will of my Father in heaven' Mt 7:21 e.g. being willing to love our enenmies and to pray for those who persecute us. (cf Mt 5:44) As someone has observed, we are no closer to God than we are to our enemy.

A Summary of the Good News

In the light of points like these surely Catholics and Protestants alike need to ask themselves, the following three questions, either in biblical terms like these or in a more contemporary way that would make more sense to the people of our day. What is the good news of salvation? Secondly, is it good news for you personally? Thirdly, how would you express that good news in concise, relevant down to earth language? For my own part I would attempt to answer the questions in the following way.

We are all sinners who have been influenced by the spirit

of evil. But Jesus has shown us, particularly by his death on the cross, that there is no need to be afraid of God's justice or his punishments. Though very real, they are on hold so to speak, until the day of judgement. Meantime we live in the age of God's unrestricted and unconditional mercy and love. So if we acknowledge our sins with a sorrowful purpose of amendment and look only into the eyes of God's mercy, expecting only mercy, we will receive only mercy, now and at the hour of our death. Afterwards we will rise to see the Lord, not as in a glass darkly, but face to face forever.

Over the years, this good news message has filtered down from my head to my heart. As it has done so, it has progressively banished the unholy fear of God that I used to experience. Instead it has provided me with the power in Paul's words, 'to grasp how wide and long and high and deep is the love of Christ, and to know this love that surpasses knowledge' Eph 3:18-19. In the light of that inner awareness of love I know what St John meant when he wrote, 'There is no fear in love, for perfect love casts out fear; for fear has to do punishment' 1 Jn 4:18. On a number of occasions this realisation has flooded me with interior consolation and brought tears of joy to my eyes. In prayer I try to renew and deepen this sense of salvation in Christ so that I might express it in my daily life. I realise that the extent to which I fail to be merciful as God is merciful (cf Lk 6:36-39) in my dealings with others, is the extent that to which I will lose the inward ability of accepting that I am accepted by the Lord.

Salvation, Mission and Ministry

This on-going sense of being saved through union with Christ and the anointing of the Spirit, is vital and indispensable in the Christian life, for, 'unless the Lord build the house, in vain do the labourers build' Ps 127:1. Knowledge, qualifications, elbow grease and sincerity are no substitute for this awareness. As St Vincent de Paul said to one of his missioners, 'The work you are about to undertake is not just the work of man; it is the work of God. Grande Opus. It is the continuation of what Jesus Christ was given to do, and consequently human effort will end up spoiling everything if God is not involved in everything we try to do.

Neither philosophy nor theology, nor preaching is effective where people's souls are concerned. It is necessary that Jesus Christ associate himself with us; that we work in him and he in us.'[22] Pope Paul VI seemed to echo these sentiments when he wrote, 'The techniques of evangelization are valuable ... But the most careful preparation by a preacher will be of no avail without the Holy Spirit and no discourse will be capable of moving people's hearts unless it is inspired by him. Without him the most skilful plans of sociologists will prove valueless.'[23] Surely these words are of crucial importance in the contemporary Church.

In recent years I have had the opportunity of working with some of Ireland's Gypsies, known as the travelling people. To my surprise, I have discovered that when there are no 'settled' people like myself around, many of them speak their own private dialect. Nobody seems to be sure where it came from, perhaps it is a mixture of Irish and Norman French. In any case I was interested to discover that 'cuinye' (the phonetic spelling) is the word they use when referring to a priest. I have also noticed that while the travellers respect all the clergy, they have a special reverence for particular priests, men of power, whose prayers, unlike those of others, can be relied upon to produce results. So when they are sick, or worried about family problems, they will often travel considerable distances in order to seek out such a man. Surely, the traveller's way of looking at priests could be applied to all Christians. Although they have been baptised and may attend to their religious duties, there is little or no evidence in the lives of many Catholics and Protestants that 'the Holy Spirit has fallen on them.' (cf Acts 8:16) On the other hand there are other Christians whose lives and ministries clearly manifest the fact that they have been 'filled with the Holy Spirit and with power.' (cf Acts 10:38)

It would seem therefore, that the grace of salvation reaches maturity when we, like the apostles and disciples are anointed with the Holy Spirit. In a scholarly treatise Frs Kilian Mc Donnell and George Montague have shown that a study of the scriptures and the fathers of the Church, indicates that the grace referred to as 'Baptism in the Spirit' by Pentecostal and Charismatic Christians is an integral aspect of the sacraments of Christian initiation. It is an experiential appropriation of the graces first received in baptism and confirmation. It could be described as a religious experience that inaugerates a new and decisive awareness of the Presence, power and love of the Lord active in one's life. As a result the person has a greater desire and ability to pray from the heart, to understand the spiritual meaning of the scriptures and to manifest the love of God in his or her daily life. These changes are often associated with greater holiness of life, a lessening of emotional difficulties and the reception of one or more of the charismatic gifts. They are mentioned in 1 Cor 12; 7-12; Rm 12:6-9; Eph 4:7-14, in the *Constitution on the Church*, par 12, the *Constitution on the Laity*, par 3, and *The Vocation and Mission of the Laity*, par 24. Mc Donnell and Montague point out that baptism in the Spirit belongs to the sacramental inheritance of all those who are sacramentally initiated into the church. 'Indeed,' they say, 'the baptism in the Spirit is normative.'[24]

Only a vivid experience of this kind can provide people engaged in mission or ministry of any kind, with both the desire and the power to witness to the good news of God's unconditional love, with courage, conviction, credibility and consistency. The extent to which it is lacking, is the extent to which the well intentioned efforts of people like priests in pulpits, teachers in classrooms and parents in homes will fail to bear fruit.

The kerygmatic proclamation has to be demonstrated in deeds of mercy and compassion. As Paul said, it is a matter of 'faith expressing itself through love' Gal 5:5. While there are countless ways of doing this, I'd suggest that the following four are important. Firstly, by forgiving those who have caused us hurt or injury.[25] Secondly, by working for reconciliation between churches and of people within churches. Thirdly, by engaging in works of charity which could benefit people, especially the poor, the marginalized and the victims of oppression. Fourthly, by engaging in action for justice by identifying and changing those structures of society which tend to perpetuate systemic forms of evil. For more on this subject see section three below.

Philanthropic action of any kind, which may appear to be good in itself, can be rooted in conscious or unconscious motives such as guilt, a need to be needed, a desire to create a good impression, unacknowledged feelings of inferiority, envious anger etc. The extent to which it fails to be the expression of an awareness of God's unrestricted love, is the extent to which it will fail to usher in the kingdom of God, which St Paul described as a kingdom of 'righteousness, peace and joy in the Holy Spirit,' Rm 14:17, or have any real significance as a form of Christian witness.

How to Grow in Saving Faith

Besides receiving the sacraments with devotion, one can renew and deepen one's faith by means of scripture reading and personal prayer. We will take a brief look at each in turn. As the bible itself says, 'All scripture is inspired by God ... it is useful for teaching the truth, rebuking error, correcting faults, and giving instruction for living' 2 Tim 3:1. So personal bible study, or regular attention to the readings during Mass can increase saving faith. For example, I regularly read a little book entitled *Daily Light* . It contains a thematic sequence of scripture verses for each morning and evening of the year. They often highlight aspects of redemption in Christ. As God's word begins to find a home in my heart, I frequently find that I am deeply moved by a fresh realisation that the Lord is saying, 'I tell you, now is the time of God's favour, now is the day of salvation' 2 Cor 6:2. Needless to say, reflection on the scriptures often leads to heartfelt prayer and contemplation. They in turn strengthen my faith in salvation.

At other times I use an imaginative prayer exercise which helps me to focus specifically on the unrestricted and unconditional mercy of God. Some of these I have described elsewhere.[26] One that I have been using recently is based on the writings of St Thérèse of Lisieux. I recall her reassuring words, 'there is only one way to force God not to judge us at all, and that is to appear before him empty handed.' I then go on to tell the Lord that in spite of my intention of loving both him and my neighbour, I haven't always succeeded. Indeed, if the truth be told, I have failed badly. Then I hand him all my deeds, good and bad alike, and stand before him vulnerable, dependant and empty handed. I then recall, some more of Thérèse's words, 'Our Lord is very justice. If he doesn't judge our good actions, he will not judge our bad ones either. For those who offer themselves to love, I don't think there will be judgement at all, on the contrary, God will make haste to reward his own love which he will see in their hearts.'[27] As I look into the eyes of God in this way I seem to receive the grace of accepting that I am accepted by the Lord of love. I realise with a triumphant surge of conviction that I am not only declared not guilty and acquitted by the grace of God, the Father sees and loves in me what he sees and loves in Jesus himself.

I sometimes realise that although my sins are many and serious, there seem to have been even greater sinners in the recent and distant past e.g. Mary Magdalen. On those occasions I recall the following sentiments which are inspired by saint Therese. I imagine that I am the son of a clever doctor. I trip over a stone, fall down and break a leg. My father hurries to me, lovingly picks me up, tends to my injuries by using all his knowledge, know-how and skill. When I realise soon afterwards that I am completely healed, I show my gratitude to my dad. Clearly I have good reason to love my father! But consider another case.

My father, being well aware that there is a stone lying in my path, hurries ahead without anyone seeing him and takes the stone away. Now obviously, I as the object of his anticipatory love, fail to realise what a misfortune my father has saved me from. As a result I do not show him any gratitude and would love him less than if I had been healed by him. But if I then got to know about the danger from which I have just escaped, wouldn't I then love my father all the more?

Yes, I am a child of God, the object of the Father's providential love. He has sent his Son to redeem not the righteous, but me a sinner. He wants me to love him because he has forgiven me, not much, but all. He hasn't waited for me to love him as much as a great sinner like Mary Magdalen did. He wants me to know how he loved me with an all-embracing love, so that I will know how to love him without reserve. One way of doing this, as we shall see in the next chapter, is to trust him at all times and in all circumstances.

CHAPTER 2

Trusting Faith

The scriptures remind us that faith without good works is dead. (cf Jm 2:17) In this chapter we will see how trusting faith is really the saving kind in action. It empowers us to do God's will no matter how difficult or impossible it might seem to be. If we present the five loaves and two fish of our good intentions, the Lord, by his grace, will bless whatever efforts we are able to make. By doing so, he enables us to be effective in our Christian lives and ministries.

Trusting faith is sustained by the conviction that 'God is able to do immeasurably more can we can ask or imagine, according to his power that is at work within us' Eph 3:20. The power of God can be experienced in three ways. Firstly, it strengthens us in our weakness, thereby blessing our efforts on the Lord's behalf. Secondly, it provides for us in all our needs. Instead of worrying about personal inadequacies or worldly obstacles, we rely on the sustaining power and providence of him who cares for the birds of the air and clothes the lilies of the field. Thirdly, it not only assures us that the Lord can and does draw good from the evil that afflicts our lives, it can help us to overcome the perverse and perverting power that we call the devil. We will reflect on each of these points in turn.

The Faith that Gives Strength

Once we can say with St Paul 'I live by faith in the Son of God, who loved me and gave himself for me,' Gal 2:20, we realise that in everyday events we are called by God to, 'live by faith and not by sight' 2 Cor 5:7. It seems to me that this involves two inter-related things.

To begin with, we need to seek God's will in all the circumstances of daily life and to be guided in all things by his Spirit. We exercise trusting faith when we ask God 'to fill us with the

knowledge of his will through all spiritual wisdom and understanding' Col 1:9. As the apostle James once wrote, 'Ask (for this
spiritual perception) in faith, never doubting ... for the doubter,
being double minded and unstable in every way, must not expect
to receive anything from the Lord' Jm 1:6-9. God can reveal his
will to us in one of many different ways e.g. an inner prompting
associated with the consolation of the Spirit, a scripture text, providential circumstances etc.[28] Secondly, having received guidance
from the Lord, we exercise trusting faith by believing that the
Spirit will empower us to do what the Father has inspired us to
do. As St Paul assures us in Phil 2:13, 'God is at work in you to will
and to act according to his good purpose.'

Like many others I have suffered from what psychologists call performance anxiety. It even surfaces in my dreams. For
example, I sometimes see myself about to preach to a congregation when I suddenly realise that the microphone is dead. With
mounting fear I fiddle with switches and plugs in a desperate
effort to restore power before the people get fed up and leave the
church in frustration. It raises the question, whose power do I
depend on in my work, my own or that of the Lord?

A few years ago I had to face this kind of dilemma in reality. We were conducting a mission in a Dublin parish. I wasn't
feeling well as I was suffering from high levels of stress and emotional fatigue. On one of the days – it happened to be my fortieth
birthday – I was relieved to find that I was neither the appointed
preacher or celebrant for that night. However, a few moments
before the eucharist was due to begin I was asked to preside for
reasons I cannot now remember. What I do recall, is the feeling of
powerlessness and emptiness I felt. Standing at the vesting bench
I said a quiet prayer under my breath, 'Lord I am at the end of my
tether, I am completely drained, I have nothing to offer. How can I
lead your people in the celebration of the eucharist? Unless you
help me, my efforts will be in vain.'

With that, we processed on to the sanctuary and the Mass
began. After a colleague delivered the homily, I approached the
altar to begin the offertory prayers. Once again a feeling of powerlessness came over me. I silently repeated the words I had
expressed in the sacristy, and proceeded with the blessing of the

gifts. As I read the eucharistic prayer something happened. I became palpably aware of a mysterious Presence. I was so moved by this consoling experience that for a moment I couldn't speak. During the pause I was amazed to find that there was an uncanny silence in the Church. There wasn't a sound. No one was coughing, shuffling or rustling paper. Evidently, everyone was aware of the Presence. When I regained my composure, I said, 'I'm sure you can all sense it, the Holy Spirit has come upon all of us, the risen Lord is here.' As I continued with the Mass the sense of Presence deepened. It was one of the most wonderful spiritual experiences of my life.

When the eucharist ended, there were unusually long queues outside the confession boxes. When people came in they said such things as, 'what on earth happened out there tonight?... That was the happiest half hour I have ever experienced in my life... I wish it could have gone on and on... I feel that God has taken away many of my fears and given me his peace instead.'

What a paradox! When I was at my lowest ebb from a human point of view, I was granted one of the greatest blessings of my entire priestly ministry. Besides being the best birthday present I ever received, it taught me a number of things. If we are seeking to follow God's will, and to minister in his name, there is no need to be afraid. If we trust in his goodness and love we discover that his 'grace is sufficient for us, for his power is made perfect in weakness... I can do everything through him who gives me strength' 2 Cor 12:9; Phil 4:13. Nowadays, when I face similar crucifixion points of powerlessness in my life and ministry, instead of anxiously wrestling with my fears, I try to prayerfully nestle in the Lord through faith. As a result, I find that I am increasingly sustained by the conviction that, 'the Lord blesses those who put their trust in him' Jer 17:7.

Faith that God will Provide

Besides relying on God's power to strengthen them in weakness, people with trusting faith are convinced that if they concentrate on trying to carry out God's will, somehow or other, in a non magical way, he will provide. As Jesus promised, 'Strive first for the kingdom of God and his righteousness, and all else will be added to you as well' Mt 6:33.

I experienced the truth of our Lord's words when I was on retreat in London a few years ago. On the evening of the second day one of my brothers phoned me, to say that our mother had just died unexpectedly in Dublin. He also mentioned that we were facing a practical problem. Another of our brothers was in France or Spain on a camping holiday, so there was no way of contacting him to tell him either about mum's death or the funeral arrangements. The question arose, would we delay the funeral for ten days until he returned, or go ahead without him?

I went to the chapel in a state of shock. As I knelt before the tabernacle in tears, a line from morning prayer in the Divine Office drifted into my mind. Some words from the book of Job had made a strong impression on me. 'Naked I came from my mothers womb, and naked I shall return. The Lord gives, the Lord takes away, blessed be the name of the Lord ... If we accept happiness from the Lord's hands must we not accept sorrow also?' Job 1:21; 2:10. I felt a strong sense of identification with these sentiments. Immediately, I decided to accept God's will by offering my mother back to the Father in a prayer of sincere thanksgiving. It had a paradoxical effect. Although I still felt shocked and sorrowful at one level of awareness, at another I felt strangely at peace. Now that I was without an earthly mum or dad, I felt a consoling sense of closeness to God, my heavenly parent, so to speak.

In the light of that experience, I began to think about the issue of my mother's funeral. It struck me that we couldn't wait until my brother returned from holidays. Then I wondered what my mother would have wanted herself. I got a strong feeling that she would have desired my brother to be there, not for her sake, but because it would be good for him. I also had a growing impression that this would also be the loving will of God. As Jesus once said, 'If you parents bad and all as you are know how to give good gifts to your children, how much more will your Father in heaven give you whatever you ask of him' Mt 7:11. So I said, 'Heavenly Father, I need your help. With confidence in your repeated promises to answer prayer, I thank you that somehow or other you will use circumstances - even apparently unfortunate ones - to bring my brother back to the funeral on time.' As I said this prayer, I had a quiet conviction that all would be well.

When I returned from London we tried to contact my

brother, in the belief that God helps those who try to help themselves. But all to no avail. No one knew where he was. I wasn't
really worried. We brought mum's remains to the church, and
still there was no word. Then around eleven that night the phone
rang. It was a friend of my brother's in London. Providentially, as
it turned out, we had been in touch with him earlier in the day to
see if he knew anything. 'You won't believe this,' he said, 'but
your brother called here earlier this evening. Apparently one of
his children was involved in a minor accident. She is perfectly
O.K. now, but your sister in law got such a fright that she decided
to return home immediately. I have given your brother the sad
news of your mother's death and he is trying to make it to the boat
at Holyhead tonight.' For my part, I felt pretty sure that he would.

Next morning we set off for the Church. There was still
no sign of my brother. As I came out on the sanctuary to begin re-
quiem Mass, a side door opened, and in walked my brother and
sister in law. Once again I felt consoled and strengthened by a
strong sense of God's closeness and love in the midst of vulnerability and sorrow. I hadn't trusted him in vain. He had been true
to his promise to answer the prayer of faith. In his providence he
had helped the family at its crucifixion point of powerlessness by
using what looked like an unfortunate incident, to bless us all.

The whole episode taught me as never before that if we
focus conscientiously on trying to do God's loving will to the best
of our ability, we can trust him to supply whatever is lacking.
When one reads the lives of saintly men and women who have accomplished great things for God, one invariably finds that they
were inspired and sustained by this kind of faith. When Cecil Kerr
of the Christian Renewal Centre in Rostrevor and Sister Consilio
of the Cuan Muire rehabilitation Centres, were embarking on
their respective projects, they had to rely on God's providence.[29]
This sense of dependence not only informed their efforts, it gave
them the assurance that God would supply whatever was lacking. As each of them dedicated themselves to following God's will
in a spirit of trust, the money and material things they needed,
simply came their way, sometimes in the most remarkable circumstances. It seems to me that only those who have trusting
faith in the providence of God, dream dreams and see visions that
translate into audacious action of a practical and fruitful kind.

The Assurance that God will Overcome Evil

Over the years I have come to appreciate that there is another type of trusting faith. Like our forebears, we ourselves and the people we care about will become the victims of all kinds of misfortune. As Barbara Ward and Rene Dubos have written, 'The actual life of most of mankind has been cramped with back-breaking labour, exposed to deadly or debilitating disease, prey to wars and famines, haunted by the loss of children, filled with fear and the ignorance that breeds more fear. At the end, for everyone, stands dreaded unknown death.'[30] Besides these external evils, there are also our own weaknesses and sins. It is important that we look at evil of all kinds from the point of view of our faith in God, rather than looking at faith in God from the point of view of evil. The latter approach tends to weaken our confidence in the Lord, whereas the former strengthens the conviction that no matter what form evil takes, it will never have the last word. Since the victorious death of Jesus on the cross, that word belongs to God. He can bring good out of all the evil circumstances of our lives. They are embraced and transcended by his plan of salvation. The Easter liturgy acknowledges this fact. When speaking of original sin and its disastrous effects it says, 'Oh happy fault, O necessary sin, that won for us such a great Redeemer.' St Paul expressed the same triumphant faith when he wrote, 'God has imprisoned all in disobedience so that he may be merciful to all ... where sin abounds, there the grace of God more abounds' Rm 11:32.

We can no more rid the world of evil than an oyster can rid itself of the grit that has entered its inner life. But just as the oyster can transform an alien presence by forming a beautiful pearl around it, so the Lord can transform the presence of evil in our lives by the all embracing action of his grace. Paradoxically, the greater the evil, the greater the pearl that is finally revealed. (cf Mt. 13:45) Pope John Paul I had this notion in mind when he said, 'I run the risk of making a blunder, but I will say it: The Lord loves humility so much that sometimes he allows serious sins. Why? In order that those who committed these sins may, after repenting, remain humble. One does not feel inclined to think oneself half a saint, half an angel, when one knows that one has committed serious faults.'[31]

It was probably an intuition like this that inspired St Paul to say, 'Give thanks in all circumstances for this is the will of Christ Jesus for you' 1 Thess 5:18. We thank God not for all circumstances e.g. cancer, alcoholism, marital infidelity, a moral weakness, premature death etc. but rather in all circumstances. We do this at all our crucifixion points of powerlessness in the firm belief that somehow or other, God will finally bring good out of evil, either in this life or in the next. As scripture assures us, 'all things work for good with those who love God' and put their faith in him. (cf Rm 8:28) If our Christian lives are informed by this kind of trusting faith we will tend to engender Christian hope in the hearts of those we meet. As G K Chesterton wrote in his *Ballad of the White Horse*,' 'Those marked with the cross of Christ go gaily in the dark.'

In our daily lives we all of us have to contend with the mystery of evil that is called the devil.[32] As we shall see in section three it can impinge upon our own lives, the lives of people we care about and upon the structures of church and state. Hans Kung has written, 'Certainly the power of evil, as it finds expression in all its menace in the life and death of Jesus, should not be minimized even today ... In the light of both the New Testament ('principalities and powers') and of modern sociological conclusions ('anonymous powers and systems'), evil as power is essentially more than the sum total of the wickedness of individuals.' [33]

I used to sense this kind of evil in a recurring dream. I'd feel threatened by an insidious presence that was so terrifying that it would leave me speechless. I'd anxiously think to myself, 'If only I could say the name of Jesus, this evil would go away.' Then I would struggle to utter the Holy Name. At first, I would only manage to whisper it with difficulty. Then I'd be able to say it. When finally, I could shout it out with defiant conviction, the sense of evil would evaporate completely. The same is true in our waking hours. The Lord can deliver us from evil, not necessarily the kind that can kill the body, but the kind that can end up as Jesus said, 'with the body and soul being destroyed in hell' Mt 10:28. As the scriptures assure us, 'The one who is in you, (i.e. the Spirit of God) is greater than the one who is in the world (i.e. Satan)' 1 Jn 4:4. No matter what temptation comes our way, we can learn to resist by relying in our crucifixion points of power-lessness, on the name and the power of the Lord. (cf 1 Cor 10:13) This kind of faith becomes a spiritual shield that 'quenches all the fiery darts of the evil one' Eph 6:16.

While most of the problems we encounter in pastoral ministry are merely human e.g. of a psychological, social or eco-nomic nature, occasionally they are due to spiritual oppression of an unusual kind. If we discern that 'Our struggle is not against en-emies of blood and flesh,' Eph 6:12, we can trust the promise of him who said, 'These signs of power will accompany those who believe; by using my name they will cast out demons' Mk 16:17. It authorises Christian men and women who have discerned the presence of an evil spirit, to perform simple as opposed to solemn exorcisms. As St Alphonsus Liguori points out, 'private exorcism is lawful to all Christians.'[34] Solemn exorcism on the other hand is rightly reserved to someone appointed by the bishop.[35] So whenever we suspect that a person's problem involves more than a psychological pathology, we can silently pray in words like the following, 'In the Name of Jesus Christ, unholy spirit, I command you to depart from this creature of God.' In my experience both in and out of the sacrament of penance, such a prayer of deliverance can be effective if it is prudently offered in a spirit of expectant faith.[36] It is uttered in the knowledge as Paul says, that we do not wage war according to human standards; 'for the weapons of our warfare are not merely human, but they have power to destroy strongholds (of evil) and every proud obstacle raised against the knowledge of God.' (cf 1 Cor 10:4-6)

How to Grow in Trusting Faith

Erik Erikson has shown in his eight stage profile of hu-man development that in its first year an infant has to learn whether to trust or mistrust itself, the world and the people who care for it. The degree to which it does so will be determined by the quality of the caring it experiences. The extent to which it is consistent, adequate and accepting is the extent to which the child's trust will be fostered and visa versa. In other words the disposition of trust is evoked in the child rather than being willed by him or her. Erikson says that the level of childhood trust car-

ries forward into adult life. Fortunately it can be changed by intimate relationships of a positive kind. For example if a mistrustful
young man falls in love and marries a good woman, her consistent kindness, respect and understanding may eventually evoke in
him a new ability to trust.

The situation is much the same in terms of our relationship with God. Because our image of deity is largely determined
by experiences of caring in childhood, we will tend to trust or mistrust the Lord in much the same way that we have learned to trust
or mistrust ourselves, other people and the world about us. However, just as positive experiences of adult love can change all that,
so a positive experience of the God of love and the love of God can
evoke a new found capacity for religious trust within us. That is
why it is so important to seek the face of the Lord and to ask him
to reveal his presence to us, thereby giving us a deep interior
knowledge of who God is and what God is like. Our desire will be
answered if we pay prayerful attention to the Lord as he manifests himself to us through things like relationships, nature, art
and especially the scriptures.

Over the years I have found that my trust in the Lord is
increased by contemplating the good news of his wonderful providence in the bible. Time and time again, it shows how God has a
plan for everybody's life, and how he can use everyday events, no
matter how negative and painful they might be, to achieve his loving purposes for us. I may say in passing that any form of reliance
on occult sciences which seek to know and to control the secrets of
the future, are alien to this sense of reliance on God and his providence. In this regard, we would do well to ponder the words of
Jesus in Lk 12:22-29, 'I am telling you not to worry about your life
and what you are to eat, nor about your body and how you are to
clothe it.' In this text Jesus shares his unshakable conviction that
God the loving Father provides for all his creatures, especially for
his own adopted children. As this truth begins to take hold of our
hearts, our trust in the Lord goes from strength to strength. We
can express and deepen our trust in divine providence by praying
the 'Prayer of Abandonment' of Charles de Foucauld:

Father I abandon myself into your hands,
Do with me what you will.
Whatever you may do, I thank you.

I am ready for all, I accept all.
Let your will be done in me, and in all your creatures.
I wish no more than this O Lord.
Into your hands I commend my spirit.
I offer you all the love of my heart,
For I love you Lord, and I give myself,
Surrender myself into your hands without reserve,
With boundless confidence, for you are my Father.

CHAPTER 3

Faith to Move Mountains

Beside the saving and trusting forms of faith we have already examined, there is a third type which can be referred to as charismatic, or mountain moving faith. Whereas all Christians need to
have the first two sorts of faith, if they are to grow in holiness,
they do not need the charismatic variety in order to do so. Indeed
St Fulgentius wrote,[37] 'The Holy Spirit can confer all kinds of
gifts (e.g. the charism of faith) without being present himself; on
the other hand he proves that he is present by grace when he gives
love.' Normally however the charism is granted by God, to those
who are already exercising saving and trusting faith in their lives.
Like any extraordinary gift of the Spirit, it is rooted in love, expresses love and is intended to build up that same love in the
community. Like any gift of the Spirit, the charism of faith is only
entrusted to some members of the Christian community. They receive it on behalf of the entire body and have a responsibility to
use it humbly, as one of the Vatican Council document puts it, for
the up-building of individuals and the Church. [38]

The charism of faith is mentioned by Paul in 1 Cor 12:9
and again in 1 Cor 13:2. He indicates that it is the key to exercising
what can be called the gifts of power such as the ability to heal the
sick, perform miracles and to drive out evil spirits. They are the
good news in action with an ability in the words of Paul VI to,
'win the attention and astonishment of the profane and secularised world.'[39] The apostle Paul said that his preaching did not
depend on arguments drawn from human philosophy but on a
'demonstration of the Spirit and power' 1 Cor 2:4. Writing about
this unusual kind of faith St Cyril of Jerusalem explained to his
catechumens,[40] 'Charismatic faith, in the sense of a particular divine grace conferred by the Spirit, is not primarily concerned with
doctrine but with giving people powers which are quite beyond
their capability. The person who has this kind of faith will say to
the mountain, 'move from here to there,' and it will move, and

anyone who can in fact say these words through faith, and believe without hesitation that they will come to pass, receives this particular grace.' Writing about the charisms of faith and power mentioned in 1 Cor 12, St Thomas Aquinas states that the preacher of the gospel should preach as Jesus did, confirming the message either through healings and miracles or by living such a holy life that can be explained only by the power of the Spirit. If we preach the power of Jesus to save and redeem the whole person, people want to see that power made real.[41] I believe that this point is particularly relevant in an age of transition when people in a secular culture find it hard to believe.

Jesus on the Charism of Faith

It has often occurred to me while reading the gospels, that it was usually the charism of faith, that Jesus commended in the lives of people he met. Scripture scholars seem to confirm this impression. Gunther Borkman has written, 'there can be do doubt that the faith which Jesus demands, and which alone he recognises as such, has to do with power and with miracle.'[42] Norman Perrin seconds this opinion when he writes, 'many of the most characteristic sayings about faith in the gospels are associated with miracles, especially healing miracles, and critical scholarship has found this aspect of the tradition very difficult.'[43] For example, when the centurion asked Jesus to help his dying servant, he showed remarkable faith when he said, 'Lord I am not worthy to have you come under my roof, but only speak the word and my servant will be healed.' Jesus was so impressed by the soldier's unquestioning confidence in his ability to heal, that he exclaimed, 'Truly I tell you, in no one in Israel have I found such faith' Mt 8:8;10.

On more than one occasion Jesus admonished the apostles for their lack of this kind of faith. For example, when the storm blew up on the lake and the apostles were scared of sinking, they roused their sleeping companion, 'Lord, save us!' they cried, 'We are perishing!' Mt 8:25. With magisterial authority, Jesus calmed the sea with a word, and turning to the apostles he said, 'Why are you afraid, you of little faith?' Not content with the saving and trusting faith they had desperately exercised, he evidently expected them to have such confident belief in God that it would have amounted to the charism of faith. They could have exercised that particular gift in either of two different ways.

Firstly, they could have exercised trusting faith of an unshakeable kind, by letting Jesus sleep on, while relying completely on the providential care of God the Father to enable them, and their precious Passenger, to ride out the storm and so to come safely to port without sinking. Secondly, they could have recalled the words of Ps 106:23-30, 'They cried out to Yahweh in their distress, he rescued them from their plight, he reduced the storm to a calm, and all the waters subsided, and he brought them, overjoyed at the stillness, to the port where they were bound.' Inspired by this verse, they themselves could have said to the wind and waves, 'In the name of the Lord, be still, be calm,' while believing that by the power of God it would happen.

Jesus spoke about the need for charismatic faith and also about it's nature. For example, when the apostles, unlike their master, failed to exorcise a young boy, they asked, 'Why could we not cast it (the spirit) out? to which Jesus replied, because of your little faith. For truly, I tell you, if you have faith the size of a mustard seed, you will say to this mountain, 'Move from here to there,' and it will move; and nothing will be impossible for you' Mt 17:19-22. Another time, Jesus cursed a fig tree which had failed to bear fruit. The following morning when Peter drew attention to the fact that it had withered overnight, the Lord replied, 'Have faith in God.' Apparently a more literal translation would read, 'Have God's faith' i.e. the special gift that only God can give. Then straightaway he went on to say, 'Truly I tell you, if you say to this mountain, 'Be taken up and thrown into the sea,' and do not doubt in your heart , but believe that what you say will come to pass, it will be done for you. So I tell you, whatever you ask for in prayer, believe that you have received it, and it will be yours' Mk 11:22-25. A number of points can be made about this astounding promise of Jesus.

Characteristics of Charismatic Faith

Firstly, we will have faith in God's promises to the extent that we have faith in the God of the promises. Through saving and trusting faith we learn what the Father is like. We recognise that he loves us so much that he would want to bless us. As St Paul said, 'If God has given us his Son would he not give us all things in him' Rm 8:32. He is the one who in his boundless generosity says to us, 'All I have is yours' Lk 15:31. Jesus referred to this intuitive awareness of God's loving impulses when he said, 'If you who are evil know how to give good gifts to your children, how much more will the Father in heaven give good gifts to those who ask him!' Mt 7:11. You could read this paragraph rather quickly and fail to appreciate just how important it is for an understanding of charismatic faith. Unless a person is anchored in a heartfelt awareness of the fact that all forms of human love, no matter how wonderful, are only pale reflections of the boundless love of God, he or she will not have the confidence to move mountains in God's name

Secondly, as far as I am aware, there is only one place in the scriptures where we are told how the different kinds of faith can grow. 'Faith,' as we note in chapter eleven below, 'comes by hearing the word of God' Rm 10:17. What St Paul is referring to here is either a particular word of revelation that jumps off the page of scripture, alive into the heart, or what charismatics call a 'word of knowledge' i.e. a gratuitous hunch or insight of an intuitive kind, for example knowing at a healing Mass that the Lord wants to heal a man in his fifties of cancer of the bladder. Like the proverbial two edged sword, a word of either kind is alive and active, going where no other word can go, 'to judge the secret thoughts and emotions of the heart' Heb 4:12. In whatever way it comes, it evokes the mustard seed of inner certainty that is characteristic of charismatic faith, while providing the power to do what it says. As the Lord reminds us, 'So shall my word be that goes out from my mouth; it shall not return to me empty, but it shall accomplish that which I purpose, and succeed in the thing for which I sent it' Is 55:11. There is an example of such an empowering word in Matthew's account of how Jesus walked on the water.

At first the apostles were terrified when they saw the Lord. 'Take courage!' he said, 'It is I. Don't be afraid. Then Peter who realised that trusting faith wasn't enough in the circumstances, replied, 'Lord, if it is you, tell me to come to you.' It is then that Jesus spoke the single word that could evoke mountain moving faith, when he said to Peter, 'come.' As long as Peter relied solely and entirely on Jesus and his word, he could walk on water. But as soon as he began to focus on gravity, wind and waves, he started to sink. As a result, he lost the grace of the present moment, regressed to trusting faith, and had to cry out, 'Lord, save me!' Having reached out to rescue him, Jesus admonished Peter for his lack of charismatic faith. 'You of little faith,' he exclaimed, 'why did you doubt?' Mt 14:22-34. It seems to me that he might want to ask his modern day disciples 'You faithless and perverse generation ... When the Son of Man comes, will he find faith on earth?' Mt 17:17; Lk 18:8.

Thirdly, people with trusting faith of the non charismatic kind, believe that the promises of Christ are true with their minds. But in everyday situations, e.g. praying for a relative suffering from cancer, they find it hard to trust the promises with their hearts. As the late Kathryn Kuhlman, who was well known for her remarkable healing ministry, once said, 'There are many who mix the ingredients of their own mental attitude with a little confidence, a little pinch of trust, a generous handful of religious egoism, quote some Scripture, add some desire – then mix it all together and label it faith ... We have formed the habit of trying to appropriate by belief, forgetting that belief is mental – faith is from God ... Faith as God himself imparts to the heart is spiritual, It's warm. It's vital. It lives. It throbs. Its power is absolutely irresistible when it is imparted to the heart by the Lord.'44 Trusting faith of the non charismatic kind prays in the hope that God may do something in the future, if what is asked is in accordance with his will. It is hedged about with if's, but's and maybe's. Significantly, Jesus never said to anyone, 'Your hope has saved you or made you well!'

Heartfelt faith of the charismatic kind that Jesus admired, is so sure of God's promises that it prays with the conviction that the Lord is doing something in the present. This kind of faith is clearly adverted to in 1 Jn 5:14, when he states, 'This is the confidence we have in God, that if we ask anything according to his will, he hears us. And if we know he hears us in whatever we ask, we know we have obtained the requests made of him.' Instead of having to see evidence in order to believe, this kind of faith believes in order to see. It's future hope is rooted in present conviction. As the letter to the Hebrews puts it, 'Faith is the assurance (in the present) of things hoped for (in the future), the conviction (in the present) of things not seen (in the future)' Heb 11:1. Derek Prince has rightly pointed out, 'Hopes that are based on true faith in the heart will not be disappointed. But without this basis there is no assurance that our hopes will be fulfilled.' 45

Fourthly, it is clear that people are only empowered to pray or to exercise charismatic faith in so far as they are consciously 'guided by the Spirit,' Gal 5:18 to act in accord with God's will. What is involved here is 'knowledge and full insight that determines what is best,' Phil 1:9, i.e. an immediate, intuitive rapport with what God wants, rather than some abstract or notional conception of the will of the Lord. To exercise charismatic faith, Christians need to develop a growing sensitivity to the nuances and subtleties of the Spirit's guidance in the concrete, here and now circumstances of life and ministry. I have dealt elsewhere with this all important subject. 46

A Case Study

For example, a nun rang recently. She asked if she could bring one of her companions to see me because she was suffering from a chronic back complaint. I reluctantly agreed. When they arrived, the sister who had arranged the meeting explained that as I preached at a conference a week or so previously, she had become convinced that if I prayed for her friend, she would recover. For my part, I was very sceptical. I suspected that it was a case of wishful thinking. But as I listened to the sister speak with such obvious compassion about the woman with the bad back, I had a growing sense that her desire for healing seemed to have been prompted by the Spirit, and was therefore, a manifestation of God's will.

As I encountered, what was yet another crucifixion point of powerlessness, I had an inner conviction – though not a strong one – that the sister could recover. As a result of many such experiences I would say in retrospect, that my level of conviction would only have scored a five, on a scale of one to ten. There have been other occasions when I would have given such an inner conviction a score of eight or nine out of ten. In any case, I felt on this occasion That I should administer the sacrament of the sick. As St James has reassuringly promised, 'Are any among you sick? They should call the elders of the church and have them pray over them, anointing them with oil in the name of the Lord. The prayer of faith (charismatic faith) will save the sick, and the Lord will raise them up' Jm 5:14-16.

To cut a longer story short, I anointed the sister with the bad back. As I did so I felt that the Lord was indeed working within her, planting seeds of healing grace that would bear fruit in the days to come. Thank God they did. Two weeks later the person who had been anointed, phoned me to say that her back was much better. All the pain was gone and her ability to bend backwards, forwards and sideways had returned. There was reason to believe that she, like many others, had been healed. I can say in passing that I have often been disappointed to find that some priests only expect the sacrament of anointing to enable people to bear with their suffering as a share in the suffering of Christ. They don't really expect it to bring about healing of mind or body. In the light of this lack of faith, is it any wonder, that many of the faithful resort to dubious alternatives e.g. of the New Age variety.

How to Grow in Charismatic Faith

Although St Paul refers to all of the charisms mentioned in 1 Cor 12: 7-11 as *energeo* i.e. temporary bursts of divine energy, the gifts of faith, healing and miracles are in a special sense, manifestations of the glory of God. By and large it is only when we ourselves 'receive the power of the Holy Spirit,' Acts 1:8 as a result of being baptised in the Holy Spirit, that we will be open to receive the charisms including the faith to move mountains. Kilian Mc Donnell and George Montague have pointed out that this 'energising power of the Holy Spirit, manifesting itself in a variety of charisms, is not religious fluff. Nor is it – as viewed by many today – an optional spirituality in the Church such as, among Catholics, the devotion to the Sacred Heart or the Stations of the Cross... It is the spirituality of the church. By that account it is not – let it be said clearly – the property of the charismatic renewal.'[47] So if you have not yet consciously appropriated the graces you received in baptism, you could ask the Lord to bless you in the fol-

43

lowing way. 'Lord Jesus Christ, you alone can satisfy the deepest desires of my heart. I offer you my life and my will, knowing that you will offer your life and grace to me. Forgive my sins. And now dear Lord come into my heart in a new way and baptise me in your Holy Spirit so that I may grasp as never before 'the length and breadth, the height and depth of your unrestricted and unconditional love which surpasses understanding so that I may be filled with the fullness of God.' Eph 3:19.

I have discovered, that once we are filled with the Spirit, there are a number of ways of growing in charismatic faith. First and foremost we must 'earnestly desire the spiritual gifts,' 1 Cor. 14:1 and specifically in this instance, the charism of faith. Otherwise like the other gifts, it will tend to remain latent rather than active in the Christian life. We do so by praying for it time and time again. We have already adverted to the fact that faith is evoked by hearing the word of God i.e. the alive, active, spoken word of the Lord, that leaps alive into the heart, where it elicits at least a mustard seed of complete assent.[48] Because this is so, we focus on those promises of God in the scriptures which assure us that he will answer our prayers by acting on our behalf even to the point of healings and miracles. I remind myself that a promise is a solemn undertaking to do something or other. Unlike fallible human beings God always has the intention and the power to do what he says. As St Paul has said, 'We may be unfaithful, but God is always faithful' 2 Tim 2:12.

I have also noticed that God's promises usually contain 'if' clauses. If we satisfy certain requirements, then God will do such and such. For example 2 Chron 7:14 contains four conditions and three interrelated promises, 'If my people who bear my name humble themselves, and pray and seek my presence and turn from their wicked ways, then I will listen from heaven and forgive their sins and restore their country.' Over the years I have noticed that the following six 'if's' are associated with God's promise to answer our petitionary prayers. We need to pray in the name of Jesus, (Jn 16:23) without resentment, (Mk 11:25) in accord with the divine will, (1 Jn 5:14) with perseverance, (Lk 11:9-13) in communion with others, (Mt 18:19-20) and with anticipatory gratitude. (Phil 4:6-7) When these 'ifs' are satisfied, the Lord answers our petitions. So I suspect that when we pray in Marian prayers, 'that we may be made worthy of the promises of Christ,' we are actually praying that we will be able to satisfy these scriptural requirements.

Over the years I have found that the manifestation of God's action in the lives of other people has strengthened my faith. For example, besides the deeds of power I have actually witnessed at first hand, a handful of books have made that kind of deep impression on me. It all began with *The Cross and the Switchblade* [49] by David Wilkerson. It recounted, not only the remarkable way in which this Pentecostal minister was led by God to work with drug addicts in New York City, but also the wonderful healings and miracles that were associated with his ministry. I have also found that books about Kathryn Kuhlman's outstanding healing ministry, such as *I Believe in Miracles*,[50] *God can do it Again*,[51] *Nothing is impossible to God*,[52] and *A Glimpse into Glory*,[53] have been a great inspiration. I may say in passing that my faith has also been strengthened by reading two biographies in particular, *Daughter of Destiny: Kathryn Kuhlman. ... her Story.*[54] and *St Francis of Paola: God's Miracle Worker Supreme.*[55] The latter is a faith stretching account of one of the most extraordinary wonder workers in Catholic history. While books like these don't seem to appeal to intellectually sophisticted people, they have helped to increase my desire and indeed my ability in some instances to receive the mustard seed of certain faith which is needed to move mountains.

Faith and the Eclipse of God

Up to this point I have given the impression that if we trust in the Lord during our crucifixion points of powerlessness, we will inevitably experience his response in one way or another. While this is normally the case, it isn't always so. We have only to look at the public life of Christ to see an example of what I mean. When Jesus depended utterly upon his Father – and he always did– the latter usually responded by revealing his divine presence and purposes to his Son's heart. Inspired and guided by the Spirit in this way, Jesus was empowered to act with unique authority, especially, by means of inspired preaching, exorcisms, healings and miracles. However, as he drew closer to Jerusalem and the conclusion of his ministry, this all began to change. Instead of feeling close to God in his hour of need, the Father's presence seemed to have been eclipsed by the dark shadow of suffering and evil. On the cross, there was nothing but silence in response to Jesus' heart rendering cry, 'My God, my God, why have you foreseken me?' Mk 15:34. For more on this, see chapter seven below.

When the leaders of the people taunted him saying, 'He saved others, he cannot save himself. Let the Christ, the king of Israel, come down from the cross now, for us to see it and believe,' Mk 15:32 Jesus was unable to respond. His usual charismatic powers seemed to have failed him, just when he needed them most. But it was at this time of desolation and powerless, more than any other, that Jesus bore witness to his unshakable confidence in the saving presence and power of God. As St Paul was to say, 'While the Jews demand miracles and the Greeks look for wisdom, we are preaching a crucified Christ: to the Jews an obstacle they cannot get over, to the gentiles foolishness, but to those who have been called, whether they are Jews or Greeks, a Christ who is both the power of God and the wisdom of God.' Paul concludes with paradoxical words which are redolent with mysterious truth, 'God's folly is wiser than human wisdom, and God's weakness is stronger than human strength' 1 Cor 1:2-26. This was clearly demonstrated, when on the third day, the Father vindicated his divine Son by raising him from the dead to glorious new life.

Following a time of felt relationship with the Trinity, individuals and groups can temporarily experience the silence and absence of God. Throughout the ages spiritual writers have argued that the Lord allows this to happen in order to purify our faith by weaning us off inadequate concepts and images of deity, with their associated feelings of consolation. He does so for the simple reason that no matter how refined our thoughts or images might be, they are quite incapable of doing justice to the incomprehensibility of the divine mystery. For example, writing of the individual's experience, Walter Hilton wrote, 'It is much better to be cut off from the view of the world in this dark night, however painful this may be, than to dwell outside occupied by the world's false pleasures ... For when you are in this darkness, you are much closer to Jerusalem than when you are in the false light.

Open your heart then to the movement of grace and accustom yourself to dwell in this darkness, strive to become familiar with it, and you will quickly find peace, and the true light of spiritual understanding will flood your soul.'[56] During the Middle Ages, Christian's seemed to be predominantly aware of God's presence. That has changed in the modern era. As Ronald Gregor Smith has written, 'The vast body of Christian people are suffering from an eclipse: they do not see the sun, they walk in shadows, and have almost forgotten what it is like to live in the splendour of light. To say that they are suffering from an eclipse means that between God and them something has been interposed. It is really God who is in eclipse.'[57]

If individuals or groups experience such crucifixion points of powerlessness, they imitate the Lord by being willing to remain in sheol as long as God would want. It is an interior state devoid of spiritual consolation. During such a time of testing and purification, individuals and groups should resist the understandable temptation to reach for idolatrous sources of consolation, whether worldly or religious. Surely this was the lesson Jesus learned as a result of his triple temptation in the wilderness, especially his inclination to throw himself from a height while relying on a spectacular miracle to save him. As Thomas Merton has warned, 'At such a time as this,' i.e. a time of desolation and temptation, 'one who is not seriously grounded in genuine theological faith may lose everything he ever had.'[58] It is an advent period when people wait patiently for the return of God. This may not occur during their individual lifetimes or that of their cultural era.[59] If that is the case, they face death like Jesus, believing that God will be faithful, by eventually raising them to the eternal glory, promised to all those who believe.

Conclusion

All of us need to grow in faith. It enables us to appropriate in conscious experience the grace of salvation which we first received in baptism. It is this awareness of the loving kindness of the heart of our God, that gives us the ability to witness to the good news. Trusting faith strengthens us in this on-going task. It also assures us that God will provide for our material needs, no matter what obstacle we encounter in trying to show his mercy and love in the wider community. Finally, while we grow in saving and trusting faith, God may choose to bless us from time to time with the charism of faith. As St Cyril of Jerusalem said, 'In so far as it depends on you, cherish the gift of saving faith which leads you to God and you will then receive the higher gift which no effort of yours can reach, no powers of yours attain.' [60]

Even a mustard seed of this gift will assure us in our crucifixion points of powerlessness, that if we act or pray in the name of Jesus, the mighty promises he made to the apostles, will be fulfilled in our lives. 'Very truly, I tell you, the one who believes in me will also do the works I do, and in fact, will do greater works than these, because I am going to the Father. I will do whatever you ask in my name, so that the Father may be glorified in the Son. If in my name you ask me for anything I will do it' Jn 14:12-15. It seems to me that contemporary forms of mission and ministry will be effective to the extent that they are expressions of saving, trusting and charismatic faith, for 'without (such) faith it is impossible to please God' Heb 11:6.

As we come to the end of the twentieth century, it is clear that our pluralistic and secularised culture is presenting the church with a tremendous challenge. Unfortunately, it seems at times that many Christians are weak in faith. They sometimes settle for defensive maintenance rather than engaging in enthusiastic mission. So instead of gaining new members, the Church is losing many of the members it already has, especially in deprived urban areas. This is a sad and ironic fact when one considers that Jesus came, as he said himself, 'to bring the good news to the poor' Lk. 4:18.

Significantly, the only Christian groups who seem to be expanding in numbers and influence at the moment appear to be those who believe in what John Wimber calls 'power evangelism.'[61] The others believe in what he calls 'presence evangelism.' It stresses the importance of incarnating faith by inculturating the good news, performing works of mercy, and taking action to achieve social justice. While accepting the importance of this approach, Evangelical, Charismatic and Pentecostal groups stress the primary need for an active proclamation of the good news which is also backed up by deeds of power such as occasional healings and miracles. While I would have some reservations about the political conservatism, the intellectual fundamentalism and the supernaturalistic tendencies of these approaches to evangelisation, it seems to me that we have a lot to learn from them. Rightly, they stress the all important role of heartfelt faith of a saving, trusting and charismatic kind.

And so, with them and the first disciples, we pray in this the decade of evangelisation, 'Now Lord, consider the threats we are facing and enable your servants to speak your word with great boldness. Stretch out your hand to heal and to perform miraculous signs and wonders through the name of your holy servant Jesus' Acts 4:29-30. As the Lord answers this prayer anew, perhaps many crows will end up singing sweetly like blackbirds, for 'what is impossible for mortals is possible for God' Lk 18:27.

PART 2

Faith and Protection from Anxiety

The nearer we come to the centre, the more we leave the images behind, the more our fears are turned into anxiety. And anxiety, if we
face it, is turned into awe. What seemed to be the power of darkness
now manifests itself as the power of light. After the great and strong
wind comes the earthquake, then the fire, and then the still small voice
1Kings 19:11-13)'

(Fritz Kunkel, *In Search of Maturity*)

CHAPTER 4

Three Forms of Anxiety

The English language is rich in words which describe a wide range of feelings and moods. In fact there are hundreds of them. For example, antagonistic, furious, hostile, outraged, scornful, quarrelsome, impatient, grouchy, defiant, sarcastic, exasperated etc. are just some of the words which are closely connected within the general family of 'angry' emotions. However, psychologists maintain that there are probably six basic emotions i.e. surprise, fear, disgust, anger, joy and sorrow. They have suggested that they are the fingerprints of subjectivity, similar in many respects to the feelings of others, but nevertheless different. This is so because they are conditioned by our unique mix of values, beliefs, attitudes and life history. Feelings are also revelatory because they disclose our subjective response to external reality e.g. to people, nature, events etc., and to internal reality e.g. memories, fantasies, dreams etc. At the deepest level of experience, feelings are our subjective responses to the intuition of values, whether aesthetical, ethical or ontological.[1] Indeed, some philosophers have argued that in the last analysis there has to be one basic emotion underlying the rest. It is the affect, that more than any other, publishes and makes known our deepest subjective response to the fact of existence.

Thinkers such as Kierkegaard, Heidegger and Sartre maintain that the perception of being, is overshadowed by the threat of non-being. As a result, a kind of dread-full fear is evoked by this awareness of contingency i.e. the fact that nothing including ourselves, necessarily exists or is the adequate explanation of its own existence. So these philosophers argue, each in their own way, that this anxious fear, not only discloses the true nature and implications of creaturely existence, it underlies all our other feelings, most obviously negative ones such as anger, disgust, and sorrow. For example if I am angry, it is because I fear some kind of of grievous loss. If I am disgusted it is because I fear the absence of a quality such as beauty or decency. If I am sorrowful it is because I fear I lack someone or something that I believe to be essential to my happiness.

On the other hand, a thinker such as Paul Ricoer or G. K. Chesterton have argued that joy is the basic emotion. It is evoked by the intuition that everything that exists, including myself, is meaningful, albeit in a contingent and limited way. It seems to me that implied in this notion are two fundamental insights. Firstly, there is the intuition that God not only created everything that exists, but moment by moment sustains and guarantees its intrinsic value and meaning. Secondly, instead of being alienated like Sartre from absurd reality, there is a profound sense of being at home in the created realm, of belonging to a world that is charged with the grandeur of God. So Ricoer can say of joy that it is 'the only affective 'mood' worthy of being called ontological. Anxiety is only its underside.'[2]

In the light of these two contradictory points of view, we are faced with the question; what is the primordial emotion, is it fearful anxiety or ecstatic joy? I would argue that like Siamese twins, they are separate but inter-dependent feelings. That said, I suspect that from a purely experiential point of view, fear seems to come first where many of us are concerned. Dr Frank Lake has suggested that if a child's sense of relationship with its mother is defective during the first nine months of life, it will experience 'a progressive diminution of the power of personal being[3] to the point of total loss, that is, towards the experience of dread or identification with non-being.' We will return to this point later in the next chapter. Suffice it to say at the moment, that the perspective of those philosophers who suggest that anxiety is the primordial emotion, may have been influenced by forgotten childhood traumas. In any case it is only as we learn to overcome such anxiety by means of a growing trust in the divine Parent who reveals and affirms our inner glory, that joy begins to replace gnawing anxiety, as the foundational feeling in human life.

The Dangers of Anxiety and Fear

Over the years I have become convinced that not only is anxious fear our primordial response to life in a fallen, contingent world, it can be one of the principal enemies of the spiritual life. In the 18th. century Jean-Pierre de Caussade could write, 'anxiety and uneasiness make the soul feeble and languid and as though sick.' When it remains unresolved, anxiety tends to squeeze love from our hearts like water from a sponge. It is not surprising, therefore, that Mother Teresa of Calcutta could say that people in the developed nations are suffering from a famine of the heart, due to a lack of love. Because God's presence has to be mediated by people and things,[4] the extent to which human love is quenched by fear, is the extent to which the light of God's loving presence tends to be eclipsed. Many people end up affirming the absence of God without denying his existence. In this sense they can say, 'God is dead. ... And we have killed him.'[5] Not only is fearful mistrust the antithesis of faith, I would agree with Italian psychologist Roberto Assagioli, when he maintains that individual anxiety causes suffering and incorrect behaviour while collective fears can carry nations into war.[6] He writes, 'I think we would be justified in saying that most of the sufferings afflicting humanity are a result of fear. Fear has no boundaries or limits: it is possible to be afraid of anything!'[7] So the saying, that nothing is so much to be feared as fear itself, rings true.

Methodology

In this and the following two chapters, I will examine the nature and effects of three interrelated kinds of anxiety, existential, neurotic and phobic, together with the motives and means we have of overcoming them. Before doing so, a note about the difference between anxiety and fear. By and large, ontological as opposed to neurotic anxiety, is a generalised fear without any particular object. It causes one to be afraid of everything in general and nothing in particular. This kind of free floating apprehension is evoked by a sense of helplessness and powerlessness before the mystery of being which is threatened by non-being. It is to be mistrusted as something intimidating and unreliable. Instead of being open and receptive, anxiety inclines a person to become suspicious, especially of anything new or unfamiliar. It is interesting to note in this context that etymologically speaking, the words 'anxiety,' 'anxious,' 'anguish' and 'angina,' are closely related.

They are derived from two Latin words. *Anxietas* means disquiet, and , *angere* literally means 'to choke, or oppress.' So unless it is mastered with grace filled courage, one could say that oppressive anxiety can choke one's sense of inner and outer reality, and with them, the mediated immediacy of the ultimate reality of God. Fear whether, normal, neurotic or phobic, is anxiety which has found a voice by focusing on a particular threat such as illness, unemployment, failure, violence, heights, thunder and lightening etc.

Existential Anxiety

When I was a young man, I read a book entitled, *The Courage to Be*, by Paul Tillich. Its masterly treatment of anxiety and fear made a deep and lasting impression on me. In one particularly insightful section, Tillich suggested that existential or objective anxiety, as opposed to un-objective or neurotic anxiety, is a healthy and appropriate response to the nature of contingent reality. It is evoked by the threat of non-being and can be experienced in any of three principal ways. Firstly there is the fear of fate and death. Apparently it was a primary characteristic of the classical, Greco-Roman period. Secondly, there is the fear of guilt and condemnation. It seemed to predominate in the Reformation era. Thirdly, there is a fear of emptiness and meaninglessness. It is the underlying mood in modern times and is evident in a good deal of twentieth century painting, music, literature, theatre, cinema, philosophy etc. While each age can be associated with a particular form of anxiety the other two will also be present. We will look briefly at each of them.

The Fear of Fate and Death

Since the dawning of human consciousness human beings have been afraid of the vagaries of fate and the inevitability of their own deaths and the deaths of people they love. I was reminded of this a few years ago when my mother and I visited the ruins of Pompeii, a town which had been destroyed in 79 AD by a volcanic eruption on nearby Mount Vesuvius. As we walked the ancient Italian streets, stood in painted villas, admired statues, and explored temples, theatres and public buildings, we were constantly reminded of the inexorability of death. For Pompeii is a dead town. This was particularly obvious when we visited the impressive street of tombs and sepulchres. The inscriptions on its gravestones and monuments, like so many of those of that period, bear witness to a preoccupation with mortality. Carved on one, for example, were these cryptic words, 'I was not; I became: I have been; I am no longer: that is all.' Contemporary authors reflected this pessimistic attitude in their writings. Lucretius sadly mused, 'Everything is slowly dying and is moving towards the grave, worn out by the length of life's path,' and Pindar came to the nihilistic conclusion, 'O my soul, do not aspire to immortality, but exhaust the realm of the possible.'

Needless to say, the fear of death continues to haunt us. We encounter it in countless ways such as nightmares, the loss of loved ones, serious ill health, road accidents, natural disasters, famines, aids, wars and the like. The awareness of mortality fills us with a conscious and unconscious fear of having to step off the cliff edge of life into the dark womb of uncreated night from whence we have come. A few years ago, Arthur Koestler drew our attention to a striking new dimension to this fear. He said that if he were asked to name the most important date in the history and prehistory of the human species, he would answer without hesitation that it was the 6 August 1945.[8] He went on to explain, that the reason was simple. From the dawn of humanity until that fateful day near the end of World War II, every man, woman and child had to live with the prospect of his or her death as an individual; but ever since the first atomic bomb exploded over Hiroshima, mankind as a whole has had to live with the prospect of its extinction as a species.

More recently, environmentalists have been warning us about the combined dangers of pollution, the green-house effect and global warming. Together they could destroy life on earth, not quickly as in a nuclear war, but slowly and relentlessly over a number of generations. If that were not enough, scientists tell us that because the sun is getting larger and hotter, it is inevitable that it will eventually kill all life on earth by first heating the planet beyond boiling point and then by absorbing it back into its own fiery centre. Sometime afterwards, the sun will consume all its energy, burn itself out, and become yet another dead star in the cosmic graveyard that is space.

Because thoughts like these about the prospect of individual and collective death, evoke such acute anxiety within us, we try to avoid them as much as possible. Ernest Becker[9] and Elisabeth Kubler-Ross[10] have perceptively described the cultural and personal ways in which we do this. To a certain extent at least, I had occasion to tap into this dynamic of denial a few years ago.

On a Summer's day, I visited a large monastic site in Scotland. It was shrouded at the time, in an erie mist that had blown in from the sea. Having walked around the ruins with two friends, we explored the adjacent cemetery, which contained many graves, some of which were hundreds of years old. At one point we came across a coffin shaped hole in the ground. It had been carved from the rock and had evidently been the resting place of a medieval monk. Now it was empty and open to the sky. I wondered if it would be big enough to lie in. I decided to give it a try and asked my two companions if they would be willing to take a photograph. This they adamantly refused to do, while trying to dissuade me from going ahead with my disturbing intention. In spite of their fear and my growing nervousness I proceeded to lie down in the stony sarcophagus. It was a weird and memorable experience. As I looked up at the sky above, I thought to myself, 'Here I lie, where another priest has lain before me. In a short time, I too will be buried forever in a grave like this.' For a scary and liberating few moments, I was able to look death in the eye. Then I quickly got to my feet, stepped out of the hollow, heaved a sigh of relief, and reverted, I'm sorry to say, to my customary state of semi denial, as far as death is concerned.

The Fear of Guilt and Condemnation

Existential anxiety can also express itself in the form of guilt feelings and a fear of condemnation. From a secular point of view this kind of guilt results from people's inability to act in accordance with their consciences. As a result, they experience the sting of non-being in the moral sphere. By failing to live in the light of their highest values, they become estranged from their deepest selves and their true potential. Not surprisingly they suffer from a sense of loss and self-condemnation. From a religious point of view, the anxiety that is evoked as a result of having missed the mark, can evoke an even deeper form of fear. Like the younger Luther, the person is not so much afraid of self-estrangement as of final judgement. On the last day he or she could be found wanting by the God of perfect justice, and therefore condemned to eternal separation from his presence and love. This is a horrifying prospect. It is said that in spite of his efforts to live a good life, Luther was so terrified by this possibility that he used to writhe in anguish upon the ground, crying, 'How can I obtain a God of grace?'[11] He only experienced relief when he came to belive that he would be justified by his faith in Christ, rather than by any work or merit of his own.

Not so many years later, in spite of the fact that he seemed untroubled by moral guilt, St Francis de Sales was assailed by a similar fear of final condemnation. While a student in Paris he had been upset by the Catholic rather than the Calvinist doctrine of predestination.[12] The spectre of eternal separation from the God he loved, caused him acute anxiety for a number of months. He resolved his problem in a curious and revealing way. If he was predestined to enjoy the presence of God, so be it. If he was to be denied that great joy, so be it. In the meantime he had the opportunity to love God with all his strength. As Wendy Wright has observed, 'He was free, not in knowing, but free to love. All the rest was unimportant, for what was most essential for him was the pure love of God.'[13] In other words, Francis overcame his anxiety by willing to love God in an unconditional way that did not depend upon the hope of reward or the fear of punishment in the next life.

St Ignatius of Loyola was afflicted with equal intensity. For months he endured a harrowing bout of scrupulosity which seemed to combine existential and neurotic anxiety.[14] He tells us that, 'although he realised that those scruples did him much harm and that it would be wise to be rid of them, he could not do that himself.'[15] Indeed he admits that they tormented him so much that he was tempted to commit suicide. 'But realising' he says, 'that it was a sin to kill oneself, he shouted, 'Lord I will do nothing to offend you.' He testifies that finally, one Sunday having received communion, he realised that his morbid preoccupation with guilt and condemnation had been prompted by the evil spirit rather than the Spirit of God. In his autobiography we read, 'he decided very clearly, therefore, not to confess anything from the past any more; from that day forward he remained free of those scruples and held it for certain that Our Lord through his mercy had wished to deliver him.'[16] While conducting missions and retreats over the years, I have met many people who have experienced a similar mixture of existential and neurotic anxiety in the form of guilt, scrupulosity, and a tortuous fear of condemnation. [17]

The Fear of Emptiness and Meaninglessness

I think that Tillich is correct when he says that in the modern era, existential anxiety finds its main focus in a widespread fear of emptiness and meaninglessness. I have suggested elsewhere[18] that in recent centuries our sense of relationship to people and nature has been undermined by a masculinisation of culture. The Reformation desacralised the world of nature. Science went on to study it in a rational and detached way as an inanimate machine. Capitalism used technological know- how and its financial resources to exploit the fruits of the earth, often in a ruthless and un-caring way. Together these cultural influences have tended to sever the umbilical cord of meaning, that connects us to people and nature, and through both to our true selves and to God. The extent to which they do, is the extent to which our enjoyment of life is undermined by an anxious sense of alienation, a suspicion, that despite all appearances to the contrary, things don't make any sense in the long run. As I mentioned earlier, this nihilistic tendency is evident in many contemporary works of art, literature and philosophy. For example, the writings of Leo Tolstoy and St Thérèse of Lisieux provide us with thought provoking instances of the kind of existential anxiety which is evoked by a sense of meaninglessness.

Tolstoy's Mid-life Crisis

When he reached the age of fifty, Count Leo Tolstoy had every reason to feel content. He had a loving wife and children, was wealthy, in good health, the most celebrated author in Russia, and the owner of a 1,350 acre estate which included as many as 300 horses. And yet he was unhappy. He felt that everything he had, and everything he had achieved, were pointless. He wrote in his diary, 'You can't close your eyes in order not to see that there is nothing ahead but the lie of freedom and happiness, nothing but suffering, real death and annihilation.'[19] He was scared by death, not so much because it marked the end of life, but because it robbed life of any meaning it might appear to have.

He was fond of quoting an oriental fable which encapsulated his feelings. A man who was being chased by a tiger climbed down into a well. At the bottom he could see the gaping jaws of a fierce dragon. Because he was unable to go up or down, the unfortunate man clung to a small bush which was growing out from between the loosened stones. As his strength began to fail him, he noticed that two mice, one white the other black, where nibbling away at the roots of the bush. Before long he would fall to his death. Just then the man noticed that there were two drops of honey on one of the leaves. Having made a supreme effort to draw himself up, he licked the nectar and waited for the end. Life is much the same, thought Tolstoy. It is sandwiched between the nothingness that precedes our birth and that follows our death. If there are drops of honey to be enjoyed, such as love of family and love of literature, they lose their savour when one knows that their meaning is called into question by the annihilation of death.

In his diary, Tolstoy reveals that during his times of depression he had the impression that 'He thought he heard a sort of distant laughter. Someone was making fun of him, someone who had worked everything out beforehand long ago ... I stood there like an idiot, realising at last that there was nothing and never would be anything in life. And he thinks it's funny!'[20] He was so demoralised by thoughts like these that he was tempted to end it all by committing suicide. In fact he stopped taking his gun with him when he went out to hunt, so that, as he said himself, 'I could not yield to the desire to do away with myself too easily.'[21] Tolstoy's crisis came to an end when, having been edified by the simple faith of some peasants he knew, he overcame his rationalist doubts and recovered his childhood sense of God. The result was dramatic, 'Everything came alive, *took on meaning* (my italics). The moment I thought I knew God, I lived. But the moment I forgot him, the moment I stopped believing, I also stopped living ... To know God and to live are the same thing.'[22]

Thérèse of Lisieux's Dark Night of the Soul

In some ways, there were striking similarities between Tolstoy's mid-life crisis in the eighteen seventies and the dark night of the soul endured by Thérèse of Lisieux some twenty years later. She was dying of tuberculosis at the time. In her autobiography she talked, like Tolstoy before her, about mocking voices, and how the fear of annihilation seemed to cancel all sense of meaning. She described how she used to get tired of the darkness all around her and attempted to refresh her jaded spirits with thoughts of heaven where her hopes were fixed. But what happened? Her torment grew worse than ever; the darkness oppressing her seemed to borrow, from the sinners who lived in it, the gift of speech. She tells us that she heard it say in mocking tones: 'It's all a dream, this talk of a heavenly country, bathed in light, scented with delicious perfumes, and of a God who made it all, who is to be your possession in eternity! ... All right, all right, go on longing for death! But death will make nonsense of your hopes; it will only mean a darker night than ever, the night of mere non-existence and annihilation. ' [23]

Like Tolstoy, Thérèse was tempted to take her own life on a number of occasions. She said, 'If I didn't have the faith, I could never endure all this pain. I'm amazed that atheists don't commit suicide more often.'[24] However on September 8, 1896. she wrote a letter to a sister, Marie of the Sacred heart. In it she mentioned a vivid dream she had experienced a few months before. She went on to describe how she had encountered three Carmelite nuns, one of whom Venerable Anne of Jesus, had founded the the order in France. Having being covered by the saintly woman's veil Thérèse saw her heavenly face suffused with an unspeakably gentle light, a light it didn't receive from without but was produced from within. This memorable dream had a remarkable effect. 'My heart was filled with joy,' she says, 'the storm was no longer raging, heaven was calm and serene. I believed, I felt there was a heaven and that this heaven is peopled with souls who actually love me, and consider me their child.'[25] Even in the midst of hellish anxiety and doubt, we can meet with him who as St Paul reminds us, descended into the depths of the earth i.e. into the hell of our darkness and anxieties, and has ascended to the very heights in order to lead forth a host of captives. (cf Eph 4:8-9)

CHAPTER 5

Coming to Terms with Existential Anxiety

There are three important steps which can be taken in order to overcome existential anxiety. Firstly, we begin by allowing ourselves to experience the fearful implications of being a creature as fully as possible. Secondly, we allow this painful sense of helplessness to articulate itself in a wholehearted desire for the God who has conquered death, forgiven sin and underpinned the meaning of all things. Finally, we need to learn how to rely on the power and providence of the Father in all the circumstances of daily life. We will take a brief look at each of these points in turn.

Acknowledging the Pain of Anxiety

I have already mentioned that, no matter what form it takes, existential or objective anxiety is a healthy and appropriate response to the experience of contingency and the threat of non-being. But as T. S. Eliot has commented, 'Humankind cannot bear very much reality.'[26] We can try to escape the pain of existence in a number of ways. Speaking from a philosophical point of view Heidegger, points out that people avoid the ontological threat which is disclosed in objective anxiety by immersing themselves in an extroverted way in the world of 'things.' As Wordsworth wrote, 'The world is too much with us ... Getting and spending we lay waste our powers,' in a distracted and distracting way. For their part, psychologists like Freud have described the many defense mechanisms, such as repression, introjection, reaction-formation etc. which are employed by the mind in order to insulate itself from conscious awareness of painful and intimidating inner realisations. Other psychologists have shown how ritualised forms of obsessive behaviour, and addictions of all kinds, have much the same purpose. As a result, the inauthentic way we live can become a strategy of avoidance that separates us from our true selves.

If we avoid existential anxiety by whatever means, it

doesn't go away. It gets buried alive in the unconscious. From there it tends to distort aspects of consciousness and reappears in the form of neurotic fears and phobias. Looked at from a psychological point of view, 'Neurosis is a synonym for *non-experience*, for not being in the world as it is.'[28] Looked at from a philosophical point of view, '*Neurosis is the way of avoiding non-being by avoiding being.*'[29] This 'inner cleavage – the state of being at war with oneself,'[30] can have a number of predictable knock-on effects. While neurotic feelings of subjective anxiety and fear may have psychological causes such as traumatic experiences, they are ultimately rooted in unresolved anxiety of an objective, ontological kind. Whereas we can often stifle our feelings of existential anxiety, it is not so easy to suppress similar feelings of a neurotic nature. They will manifest themselves in the form of tension, stress, disturbed dreams, psychosomatic aches and pains etc. Although neurotics spend a lot of time trying to overcome their conscious fears, they won't have complete success until they are willing to face up to the unconscious anxiety of an existential kind, that prompted them in the first place. This point is usually overlooked by 'self-help' books and groups.

From a psychological and existential point of view it is important that we recover, name and own our worst anxieties, and that we try to understand the perceptions that evoked them in the first place. If we begin by getting in touch with a neurotic fear such as hypochondria, we need to go on, not only to identify its origin in our own particular life history, but also in the forms of ontological anxiety already mentioned. For example, a hypochondriac's fear of sickness could be rooted in memories of family illness in the past and a deep seated but unacknowledged fear of death. We need courage and humility to face such truths, courage to overcome our fear of non-being, and humility to acknowledge how helpless and powerless we are to do anything about it.

The Spiritual Potential of Anxiety

As our anxiety discloses the implications of creaturehood in this way, it puts us in touch with the poverty of spirit[31] and 'childlike need'[32] which, according to Jesus, are prerequisites for entry into the Kingdom of God. So there is more than a little truth in Schleiermacher's assertion that religion is a 'feeling of absolute dependence.'[33] It finds expression when we allow the pain and fear within us to become prayerful cry to God. As St Augustine wrote, 'The person, who, wandering in the abyss, screams out overcomes the abyss. The scream itself lifts the person above the abyss.'[34] The awareness he seems to be referring to, is implicit in steps one and two of Alcoholics Anonymous. They could be adapted to read, 'we admitted that we were powerless over our anxieties and their causes, and accepted that they had become unmanageable. And so we came to believe that only a Power greater than ourselves could deliver us from them and grant us peace of mind.' As Jung observed, 'Man is never helped in his suffering by what he thinks for himself; only superhuman, revealed truth lifts him out of his distress.' [35]

The extent to which we acknowledge our desperate need for a revelation of God's existence and saving power is the extent to which we will summon up all our energies in a concerted desire for both. To experience such desire is to have already experienced the grace of God at work in the 'sacred woundedness' of our anxiety. As Jesus acknowledged, 'No one can come to me unless drawn by the Father who sent me' Jn 6:44. If the Lord seems to delay in responding, it is only because he wants to deepen and purify our desire. But he promises, 'I know the plans I have for you ... plans for your welfare and not for harm .... when you call upon me, you will find me; if you seek me with all your heart, I will let you find me, says the Lord ... and will tell you great and hidden things that you have not known' Jer 28:1-14; 33:3. While we cannot be constantly and consciously aware of our desire for God, it can continue to inform our awareness in an unconscious way, thereby disposing us to receive revelation whenever God chooses to grant it. We have already seen how desires rooted in ontological and neurotic anxiety led Luther, Francis de Sales, Ignatius of Loyola, Leo Tolstoy, and Thérèse of Lisieux to a new found awareness of the Lord.

Desire to know God

When I was in my late teens and early twenties I endured a painful crisis of faith. For a time I doubted the existence of God and of ultimate meaning. For years I anxiously tried to resolve these issues by means of personal meditation, discussion with others, and philosophical reading. No matter how hard I tried, convincing answers seemed to elude me. Then, unexpectedly I experienced a welcome and grace filled breakthrough. I was studying for an exam at the time. Not for the first time, I happened to doze off to sleep at my desk. As I woke up there was a fleeting moment when I was conscious, but not of anything in particular. There was no idea or image in my mind. Instead, I had a vivid, direct and unmediated awareness of my sheer existence and, by extension, of the existence of all things. It was accompanied by a strong inner conviction that being, which included my own, was *good* and *meaningful* in itself, but that it wasn't the adequate explanation of its own existence or meaning. In that moment I had an intuitive assurance that God existed as the One who sustains in being all the good and meaningful things that exist, including myself.

I was interested to read how American author David Granfield says that as a young man he had a similar experience while walking through the woods. He stopped beside a low hanging branch and became fascinated by tiny leaves that had just unfurled. He touched one of them and became aware of how vulnerable it was. And nevertheless, despite all the possible dangers it had to encounter, there it was, resisting non-existence by existing. But he was aware that it wasn't the sufficient reason of its own existence. There had to be a something else, something that was sheer existence, a majestic, self-sufficient being to account for the tiny leaf's brief hold on life.

Granfield goes on to say, that by playing the same game with himself, alternately confronting his nothingness and asserting his existence, he brought the experience of the desperate need for a necessary being, an infinite ground, into the inner realm of his uniqueness and self-awareness. 'I, too, exist,' he mused. 'I, too, am a being who can not account for his own existence. I too need the infinite support of the Being who must exist, else I perish. Contemplating my own conceivable nothingness snatches me away from the ivory tower of concepts and sweeps me into moment-to-moment actuality. The divine ground is not merely through creation an historical beginning for me, it remains an indispensable presence and an infinitely desirable good. This abiding awareness,' he concludes, 'crowns security with gratitude, humility with love.'[36] Although, Granfield rightly says that such an experience can be repeated, I would be more inclined to say, that once it occurs it acts as an underlying awareness that informs our perception, especially during moments of contemplative attention to reality. Experiences of this kind have also taught me that Viktor Frankl was correct when he pointed out that human beings do not create the meaning in their lives, they progressively discover it.'[37]

Proving that God Exists

Many years ago I was interested to see that the philosopher, Jacques Maritain believes that pre-philosophical intuitions of being such as the ones I have described, convince natural reason that God exists. Maritain says[38] that the intuition of existence, grasping in some existing reality being-with-nothingness, makes the mind grasp by the same stroke the necessity of being-without-nothingness i.e. God. The whole thing is direct and uncomplicated because the illuminating power of this intuition takes hold of the mind and obliges it to see. Thus it naturally proceeds, not in a reasoned way, but in a primary intuitive flash, from one imperative certainty such as the intrinsic meaning of contingent being, to another i.e. to a spontaneous knowledge of God's existence as the One who holds all things in being.

It is this intuition that forms the basis of St Anselm's ontological argument for the existence of God. It begins with the concept of God as that than which no greater, or more perfect can be conceived in thought; and argues that there must be such a being, since to think otherwise would amount to a contradiction of supposing the most perfect conceivable being of lacking the perfection of existence.[39] The same is true of the five proofs of St Thomas Aquinas, especially the third, which is based on the experience of the contingency of being.[40] Briefly put, it goes something like this. Existing beings are generated and are subject to corruption, capable of being and not being. Since these beings can be and not be, it is impossible for them to be always. Their being, therefore, needs a cause that did not come to be but always was and is necesary i.e. God.

Without the intuition of the meaning of being, the arguments for God's existence may be reasonable, but they will never be convincing. As Maritain has said, before talking about any of them, teachers like himself should 'make sure that those we are addressing are awakened to the primordial intuition of existence and aware of the natural knowledge of God involved in it. When people have had such an intuition that they don't need to prove that God exists, they know he does.' [41]

Although, I have described my own journey to faith in philosophical terms, there are many other ways of coming to the same firm conclusion e.g. by means of a genuine religious experiences of what Rudolf Otto referred to as the numinous i.e. an awareness of the divine.[42] What is important, is the fact that we move, if needs be, from a *notional* to a *real* knowledge of God[43] as Absolute Meaning, and the guarantor of all the worldly meanings we perceive. For example, when asked if he believed in the existence of God, Carl Jung replied, 'All that I have learned has led me step by step to an unshakable conviction of the existence of God. I only believe in what I know. That eliminates believing. Therefore I do not take His existence on belief *I know* that he exists.'[44] It is this kind of heartfelt faith which banishes our existential fear of emptiness and meaninglessness. As it does, anxious mistrust begins to give way to joyful affirmation and gratitude, as the heart's deepest affective response to reality. (cf Rm 1:21) I say begins, because, until we overcome the fear of death and condemnation, anxiety will continue to undermine our lives.

Desire for the mercy of God

Although I grew to have firm belief in the God of the philosophers, I didn't know the Lord as a person. In my late twenties, I was aware of a growing desire to encounter Him in a personal way and to experience his liberating mercy and love as never before. My prayers were answered after two years or so, when I finally experienced a spiritual awakening in February 1974. As the Lord filled me with the Holy Spirit I felt that Jesus had become my second self, that my sins were forgiven and that I was loved unconditionally by God the Father. I had the grace to accept that I was accepted. It was as though a voice were saying, 'You are accepted.' *You are accepted*, accepted by that which is greater than you ... do not seek anything; do not perform anything; do not intend anything. *Simply accept the fact that you are accepted* ... In that moment, grace conquered sin, and reconciliation bridged the gulf of estrangement'[45] with its associated guilt of a moral and a psychological kind.

I have dealt with the subject of 'saving faith' at some length in chapter one above. As it suggests how people can grow in that all important form of trust, I will add very little here.[46] Suffice it to say that over the years people's awareness of the loving mercy of God can deepen and strengthen. As it does, it will tend to reveal, challenge and to displace many negative images of God which have lurked in their unconscious minds since childhood.[47] So instead of fearing God as heretofore, they will increasingly learn to trust the Father in a loving way. As St John has said, 'Love comes to its perfection in us when we can face the Day of Judgement *fearlessly.*' 1 Jn 4:17

Desire for eternal life

St Gregory of Nazianzen described the ephemeral nature of life in these poignant words, 'The life of humans my dear people, is but a fleeting moment of being alive. It is a child's game played upon the earth. A ship upon the sea that leaves no wake. The flight of a passing bird. Dust, mist, morning dew and a bursting blossom.' Sooner or later we all have to yield to the darkness of death. It is most likely to come in the form of heart disease, cancer, respiratory illness and accidents, because research indicates that these are the most common causes of death in the developed nations.

Experience has taught me that people have different reasons for fearing death. In our secular culture, many men and women find it hard to believe that there is any life other than this one. Furthermore, due to the fact that they have actually seen very few people dying, they fear death as something alien and unfamiliar. For example, although I have been a priest for over twenty years and worked in two hospitals, I have only seen one person die in all that time. Some of the adults I have talked to, say that they are not bothered by mortality itself. What scares them is the possibility of having to endure a painful sickness before they die, or having to face a harsh judgement afterwards. Still others say that it is death itself that frightens them. Although they may be church goers, they suspect that their last breath will lead to the complete and permanent annihilation of their personalities. So not surprisingly they resist death with a mixture of fear and defiance. They would identify with these words of Dylan Thomas, 'Do not go gentle into that good night. Old age should burn and rave at close of day; Rage, rage against the dying of the light.' But there are people who welcome death, either because it will put an end to the pain of having to live in this valley of tears, or because they want to see the Lord face to face in glory. That said, most of us are afraid of death most of the time. This fact raises the question; having honestly faced such a fear, how can we overcome it?

Proving the Immortality of the Soul

We could begin by looking at philosophical arguments for the immortality of the soul. They began with Plato and were adopted by Christian thinkers like St Thomas Aquinas.[48] For example Jacques Maritain has written, 'A spiritual soul cannot be corrupted, since it possesses no matter; it cannot be disintegrated, since it has no substantial parts; it cannot lose its individual unity, since it is self-subsisting, nor is its internal energy, since it contains within itself all the sources of its energies. The human soul cannot die. Once it exists, it cannot disappear; it will necessarily exist for ever, endure without end. Thus philosophic reason, put to work to work by a great metaphysician like Thomas Aquinas is able to prove the immortality of the human soul in a demonstrative manner.'[49] Many present day Christians have problems with an argument like this. Firstly, it presumes a philosophical outlook that very few people would share any more. Secondly, even if they accept that the soul is indestructible, they suspect that consciousness necessarily dies with the brain. So they ask, what is the point of being immortal if one is not aware of the fact? Although parapsychologists and spiritualists believe there is life after death because of their supposed communication with the dead, I find that their arguments are unconvincing. John Hick has pointed out that messages received at seances, for example, can be understood in terms of telepathic sensitivity to the knowledge and memories of surviving relatives and friends who are present. [50]

Resurrection and Life After Death

On one occasion St Paul declared, 'All I want is to know Christ and the power of his resurrection and partake of his sufferings by being moulded to the pattern of his death, striving towards the goal of resurrection from the dead' Phil 3:10-1. With the passage of time, I have found that as my growing desire to know Christ and his merciful love has been satisfied, I have not only been more willing to share in his sufferings in different ways e.g. through compassionate solidarity with those who are afflicted, I have also had a deepening belief, that like him, I will be raised from death to new life. In other words, while I find it hard to accept philosophical proofs for the immortality of the soul, I have a growing conviction, some of it based on a vivid prayer experience a few years ago,[51] that the God who created the world will re-create us on the last day by raising us from the dead. The letter to the Hebrews 2:14-15, assures us, 'Since all the children share the same human nature, Christ too shared equally in it, so that by his death he could set aside him who held the power of death, namely, the devil, and set free all those who had been held in slavery all their lives by the fear of death.' Needless to say, as this consoling prospect makes its home in our hearts, it helps liberate us, bit by bit, from our natural fear of death and non-being.

Over the years, I have come to the conclusion that the extent that we can return the Christian love that we have received from other people – especially family members and friends – is the extent to which we will know the unconditional love of God which is mediated in this way. I know that there have been joyful moments, in my own life, when I have looked with love into the loving eyes of friends and have had an intuitive awareness that the love we share is a participation in the eternal life of the God who is Love. (cf 1 Jn 4:8) As such, although our bodies will die, *agape* love, the love that God has poured into our hearts, will never die. As the Song of Songs 8:6-7 puts it, 'Love is as strong as death, passion as fierce as the grave. Its flashes are flashes of fire, a raging flame. Many waters cannot quench love, neither can floods drown it.' In the New Testament St Paul wrote, 'I am convinced that ... death ... will not be able to separate us from the love of God in Christ Jesus the Lord.' Rm 8:38-39 So as long as we experience that love in and through our relationships with one another, we will have intimations of eternal life. It will serve to lessen our fear of death, by witnessing to the good things that God has prepared for those who love him. (cf Mt. 25:34 & 1 Cor 2:9)

Near Death Experiences

In the mid 70's, Raymond Moody, a doctor of medicine and philosophy, published a book with the tantalising, if misleading title, *Life after Life*.[52] It contained graphic and consoling accounts of experiences which patients claimed to have had in the period following their clinical deaths and before their subsequent resuscitation by doctors. The term clinical or reversible death, is by definition a bit of a misnomer. In medical circles it refers to that critical time of four or five minutes duration, which precedes biological or irreversible death, when heart and lungs have ceased to function, and *life* is ebbing away. Strictly speaking, therefore, there are only 'near-death' as opposed to 'after-life' experiences. So, while they cannot be adduced as proof of the immortality of the soul, they can be used to take away our fear of the dying process.

Apparently, about 20% of resuscitated people can recall a near-death experience. By and large, they are positive; those who have had negative ones, seem to forget them afterwards. Moody discovered that while people's accounts differed as far as detail was concerned, there were striking similarities. A composite version of the near-death experience would read as follows.

A dying man overhears his doctor pronouncing him dead. Then he hears another disturbing sound, a loud ringing or buzzing. At the same time he feels as if he is passing through a long dark tunnel. Then he finds he is outside his body. He looks at it with mixed emotions as he watches the doctor trying to resuscitate him.

It is then that he notices that he still has a body of a kind, but it is different from the body he has left behind. Shortly afterwards he meets men and women who come to help him. He notices the spirits of deceased relatives and friends and a loving Spirit the like of which he has never encountered before – a being of light – have appeared before him. In a wordless, non threatening way, this Spirit asks him to review his life, and helps him by showing him a comprehensive video like playback of the most important events in his life. Following that, he journeys onward and finds that he is arriving at some type of borderline or frontier which apparently represents the dividing line between this life and the one that is yet to come. As he does so he feels that he must go back to the earth because the time of his death has not yet come. He is so fascinated by what is happening that he finds that he doesn't really want to return. He is filled with intense feelings of joy, love and peace. Despite his reluctance, he nevertheless finds himself reunited to his body and obliged to live his life in the everyday world.

Following his recovery, he tries with difficulty to tell other people about the inexpressible other worldly experiences he has been through. Because they joke about them with obvious scepticism he stops telling anyone about them. Nevertheless his neardeath experience profoundly affects his life. He loses his fear of death and revises his understanding of its relationship to life. By taking such testimonies seriously, people who have never had such an experience, may find that their fear of dying is reduced.

Relying on the Providence and Power of God

Life is unpredictable. We never know what the next day is going to bring. Will it be an unexpected illness such as a stroke, the death of a family member, the loss of one's job, a natural disaster such as being hit by a tree during a storm, bad news about a loved one, a humiliating failure of some kind, a traffic accident, a robbery, an assault etc? The list of possibilities is almost endless. One way or another we are 'worried and distracted by many things.' Lk 10:41 Then, if that wasn't enough, there is the relentless pace and pressure of a fast changing world to contend with. They make such demands on our nervous systems that we are inclined to suffer from stress and even burn-out, together with associated psychosomatic problems such as head-aches, high blood-pressure, depression and the like. [53]

Jesus made it clear that he didn't want fear to undermine

us in this way. He said, 'Do not worry about tomorrow, for tomorrow will bring worries of its own. Today's trouble is enough for today.' Mt 6:34 And how will this be done? We need to live in the present moment while relying entirely on the grace of God to see us through. Anxious remembrance of past events, together with fearful anticipation of possible events in the future, tend to rob us of the ability to seek God's will in the present. That is why both our memory and imagination need to be controlled and disciplined. We commend our past to God's mercy, our future to his providence and the present to his love. The gospels show how Jesus wanted us to imitate his example firstly, by being led by the Spirit and secondly, by depending on the providence and the power of God in all circumstances. As far as the guidance of the Spirit is concerned, we can say, 'Lead kindly light, lead Thou me on. I do not ask to see the distant scene, *one step* enough for me.'[54] When it comes to dependence on God, we rely on the power of his Spirit at work within us which is 'able to accomplish abundantly far more than all we can ask or imagine.' Eph 3:20 I can recall one particular experience which taught me a lot in this regard.

I was attending an eight day directed retreat in Weston Massachusetts at the time. Like my life in general it wasn't going very well. I was feeling bad about the past and was filled with a neurotic fear of doing badly on the retreat, the course I was attending, and in the future in general. On the evening of the fifth or sixth day, I lay on my bed feeling miserable. Then on impulse I knelt on the floor beside the bed and began to pray. After a few minutes or so a vivid, dreamlike image came into my mind. I was in a large, dimly lit cave. A few yards away I could see an open book resting on a rock. I thought to myself, 'great, that must be the bible, I'll go over read what it says, and receive consolation and direction from the Lord.' But when I got close to the book, I was extremely disappointed to find that the pages were blank. In a spirit of anger and desperation, mixed with longing I cried out to the Lord, 'That's typical, I see a bible and there is nothing on the pages. why have you abandoned me like this, I am sick and tired of having to listen to myself, why don't you say something to me?' As soon as I had got those sentiments off my chest, the following words seemed to come to me, 'Read Is. 41:10 and I will speak to you.'

At first I thought, 'I'll take no notice; that inspiration has probably come from my own imagination rather than from the Lord.' But when I considered how spontaneously and insistently it had occurred I decided to look for the verse in question. I flicked open the bible and glanced downwards. I was surprised and impressed to see that I was looking at Is 41. Then in verse 10, I read these memorable words, 'Fear not, for I am with you, be not dismayed, for I am your God; I will strengthen you, I will help you, I will uphold you with my victorious right hand.' Talk about the about the word of God being alive, active and relevant. It literally jumped off the page into the depths of my heart. As I savoured its meaning, I found that it was giving me the courage to face the future with confidence. After all, I had been assured that God was with me, he would uphold me at all times.

Although that verse didn't take all my fears away – they still trouble me from time to time – it changed my attitude to them. Firstly, I have come to realise that my fears do not come from God. That realisation, has become an important rule of discernment in my life. As St Paul reminds us, 'The Spirit you received is not a spirit of fear, but rather a spirit of love and power and self-control' 2 Tim 1:7. Fear comes from our human nature, and not from God. Therefore we should be guided, not by this craven, worldly spirit, but by the Spirit of God at work within us. That is why the Lord says time and time again in the scriptures, 'Do not be afraid,' Ex 14:13, 'Be determined and confident,' Jos 1:9, 'Do not be discouraged,' 2 Chron 20:15, 'Do not worry,' Mt 6:34. God means just that. His words are words of command and not of advice. When we experience fear, we shouldn't be mastered by it. Having acknowledged its presence, we should freely, and deliberately decide, that with God's help we will courageously do his will, no matter what dangers and obstacles may lie ahead. I have found that if one steps out in faith in this way, one's fears begin to abate or to disappear altogether. There are a number of concrete examples of what I mean in the section on trusting faith in chapter two above.

Transcendence and Fearlessness

While many philosophers and psychologists have interesting and worthwhile things to say about human anxiety and fear, I'm convinced that they can offer no real and lasting cure. Great spiritual teachers have taught us why this is so. They assert that the conscious and unconscious types of anxiety which trouble so many people's lives are the inevitable consequence of worldly egocentricty and a lack of transcendental relationship with God. For example Karl Rahner says that at least some of the neurotic anxiety we experience is due to the fact that we try to be simultaneously committed to Christian and to worldly values, such as a desire for riches, reputation and ethical independence. But when push comes to shove, we don't say, 'I *will not* forego such and such a thing,' but rather, 'I *cannot* forego it.' However this admission of being unable to change, is clearly a manifestation of the personality's identification with a particular good of a worldly, created kind. 'All conflicts, all neuroses,' Rahner concludes, 'are due at least partly to this fact that a person cannot really choose, cannot decide, wants to produce impossible syntheses which do not exist in this life. Christ came to bring a sword, not peace (Mt 10:34).'55 Not only is this true of individuals, by extension it is also true of groups and nations. While the vast majority of the world's people are virtually imprisoned in poverty, the affluent and largely unresponsive minority, especially in the developed nations, seem to be imprisoned by anxiety. Arguably they will only be freed from their fears when, as a result of conversion, they are willing to restore the broken bonds of fellowship by helping the dispossesed to escape from their poverty. 56

In the light of what we have been saying, it logically follows that anxiety will only be mastered, and overcome when it is displaced by means of humble, whole hearted openness to the God of love, his values and his will. In his *Perennial Philosophy*, Aldous Huxley endorses Rahner's analysis when he points out that fear, worry and anxiety are tell tale signs of self-absorption and separation from God. They cannot be overcome by personal effort, but only by the ego's absorption in a cause greater than its own interests. 'Absorption,' he adds, 'in any cause will rid the mind of some of its fears; but only absorption in the loving and knowing of the divine Ground (i.e. God) can rid it of all fear.'57 However, it can be pointed out that if we want to be open to God in this way, we need to be loving to our brothers and sisters, especially the least of them, (cf Mt 25:45; 1 Jn 4:12) as both the means and the consequence of openess to God.

Universalising Faith and Fearlessness

Since World War II, a number of writers such as Piaget, Erikson, Kohlberg, Levinson, Gilligan and Loevinger have outlined the different stages involved in human development. They did this from their own particular points of view whether, cognitive, moral, psycho-social and so on. In more recent years James Fowler has studied the transcendental aspect of these theories. He has suggested that the activity of investing faith in centres of power and value beyond ourselves, such as the person and teachings of Christ, can develop through a series of six stages. It seems to me that two of them are particularly relevant as far as our discussion of anxiety is concerned. He says that people at the fifth stage are characterised by what he calls 'Conjunctive Faith.' They go beyond the black and white, either-or distinctions which are common in the preceding stage of 'Individuative- Reflexive Faith ' to look at things in a subtle, paradoxical manner e.g. they can combine contemplative prayer with committed action for justice. Yet, a fundamental tension still remains: their urge to give themselves fully to the Lord e.g. by showing concern for the poor, can be inhibited by a fear of the possible sacrifices that might be involved. In the light of this point, it would seem that even at stage five, the conflict mentioned by Rahner can remain unresolved.

Some people, though a very small number, by all accounts move into the sixth stage of of 'Universalising Faith.' It marks the completion of a tendency that was evident in the earlier stages. 'A person decentres,' says Fowler (i.e. moves from a self-centred to an Other-centred perspective) in the valuing process to such an extent that he or she participates in the valuing of the Creator and values other beings – and being – from a standpoint more nearly identified with the love of the Creator for creatures than from the standpoint of a vulnerable, defensive, anxious creature.' He goes on to add that the self-emptying involved in Universalising Faith, 'is actually the fruit of having one's affections powerfully drawn beyond the finite centres of value and power in our lives that promise meaning and security. 'Perfect love casts out fear,' as it says in 1 Jn 4:18.' [58]

Two other researchers in particular have studied some of the characteristics of stage six people. At the end of the last century, Richard Bucke examined the lives and teachings of people who developed universalising faith as a result of what have been variously referred to as 'transcendent ecstasies,'[59] 'subliminal awareness'[60] and 'peak experiences.'[61] As a result they move from self-consciousness to what he calls 'cosmic consciousness.' Experiences of this kind tend to have some typical features. Beside happening suddenly and unexpectedly, they get rid of three things; unresolved guilt, anxious fear and doubts about future immortality. We know from the lives of the saints that they also impel Christian men and women like Vincent de Paul and Mother Teresa of Calcutta to become God's answer to the cry of the victims of injustice and poverty. For his part, Roberto Assagioli studied the nature and characteristics of what he called 'super-consciousness,' i.e. a spiritual faculty of the unconscious which enables people to have a heightened intuitive awareness of reality in a way which is usually religious in character, though not necessarily in terms of the teachings of any particular religion.

Speaking of this higher state of spiritual development Assagioli wrote, 'The experience of super-conscious reality cancels out fear, for any sense of fear is incompatible with a realisation of the fullness and permanence of life.'[62] This statement confirms Jung's well known belief that people suffering from neuroses would only manage to overcome their anxieties and fears when they recovered a religious outlook on life.[63] It should be said in this connection that Jung was referring to genuine religious experience as opposed to a merely formal adherence to a Church. He found that many of the practicing Christians who consulted him, had notional rather than real faith in the Lord. It appears therefore that the extent to which worldly, self-centred, desires and attachments are renounced in the name of a whole-hearted, commitment to the living God who is in the midst of our lives, is the extent to which existential and neurotic forms of anxiety and fear will tend to wither.

CHAPTER 6

Neurotic Fears and Phobias

We have already looked at the interrelationship between existential and neurotic forms of anxiety. In this chapter, we will look at the nature, causes and typical effects of what psychologists refer to as separation anxiety. We will then go on to suggest possible ways of overcoming this neurotic problem which afflicts so many people today.

Separation Anxiety

Apparently, when a child is born it leaves the mother's body and enters into an idyllic state of symbiotic union with her i.e. one of merged identities. While being breast or bottle fed satisfies its biological needs, the child is fed emotionally and spiritually by the quality of the mother's love, or that of a substitute carer, such as a relative or nurse. The mother may speak and caress, the baby may gurgle and smile, but basically there is no exchange of thoughts. Rather the child is en-wombed psychologically as its identity is established in the reflected light of the mother's love. Frank Lake has referred to this process as, 'being-in-relatedness.' The extent to which the carer's affirming love appears to be conditional or defective is the extent to which the child's sense of self and well being will be weakened.

Sometimes a child gets the impression that it is neither good or lovable because of being separated from its parents – especially from its mother – during the first nine months of life. There can be many reasons for this. Firstly, the child may be born prematurely. As a result it is kept in hospital, and so deprived of physical contact with its parents. Or it may be that the child has to go to hospital during the first months of its life. The parents visit, then they have to go away again. The child can feel rejected. If it does, it blames itself. It feels: 'There must be something wrong with me, that is why my parents keep on leaving me!' Secondly, it may be that the mother herself has to go to hospital for an extended period. She might even die. The child doesn't understand this. It feels deserted and abandoned. Thirdly, it sometimes happens that a sick or pregnant mother will send one of her children to stay with a grandmother or aunt. In the event, it never returns. Although it is brought up in a caring home, the child may get the impression that it was given away because it wasn't wanted. Fourthly, a child may have been adopted after it had already bonded with its natural mother. Again it can come to the emotional conclusion that it was 'given away,' because it was unlovable. Fifthly, a mother who has to go out to work because of economic necessity, may reluctantly entrust her child to a carer for a few hours, a number of days a week, during the first nine months of its life. By all accounts, because most children need to be in fairly constant visual contact with their mothers during that vital period, prolonged absences can evoke painful feelings of loneliness with detrimental knock on effects.

Even when they live at home, children can be emotionally if not physically separated from their parents. consequently they lack the kind of love which is needed to grow up with a feeling of worth and inner security. For instance, if either the mother or father is suffering from a mental problem such as depression, severe anxiety, schizophrenia etc., he or she might be unable to give the kind of affection that the child would need. In some homes the mother's emotional energies are so absorbed by the difficult task of coping with an unhappy marriage, an alcoholic husband etc. that she has very little to spare for the children. Worry about bills and possible bouts of violence can create an atmosphere of uncertainty, tension and fear in the home. Needless to say, this kind of environment tends to generate high levels of anxiety and low levels of self-acceptance. Lastly, a couple may have many children in rapid succession. As a result, one or more of them might feel neglected from a psychological point of view. This could be particularly true if the parents are inhibited when it comes to the expression of physical or verbal affection to either one another, or to their children.

Separation Anxiety and the Threat of Non-Being

Psychologists are agreed that the extent to which a child

experiences separation from the love of the mother, especially in the first months of its life, is the extent to which it will feel insecure. 'So long as the mother is present, and satisfactorily so' writes Frank Lake, 'the baby experiences its being and well-being in identification with her. It cannot conceive of life going on without her, except for short times when her coming is delayed.'[64] The infant becomes so dependent on the mother's presence that, if for some reason or other she fails to return, the power of being-by-relatedness-to-her is depleted to dangerous levels of hopelessness. A lively expectation of receiving love gives way to despair because the child's emerging sense of identity, and worth are at risk. This feeling of unlovability causes a feeling of anxiety and acute distress. Lake adds these sobering words, 'even though at this point of maximal tolerable panic the mother returns and the experience is split off and repressed, *it remains as an indelible as*pect *of personal identity.*'[65] (My italics) Not surprisingly, such painful memories are buried in the unconscious. But they continue to influence the person's feelings and attitudes in adult life, as we shall see later.

Dr Lake suggests that this childhood encounter with non-being links up with Tillich's three forms of ontological anxiety. 'In my experience, he writes, 'working at depth analysis of the first year of life,' it is clear that, 'these three forms of anxiety lie at the roots of these the three main intolerable positions into which the infant spirit can be driven, the hystero-schizoid, the paranoid and the depressive, respectively. Certainly, before the age of one year, infants can suffer from all these three anxieties, the dread of death, the persecutory anxiety of emptiness and the depressive conflict of guilt and condemnation.'[66] This observation confirms the likelihood of a link between ontological and neurotic forms of anxiety as we suggested earlier.

Anxiety and the Super-Ego

A child is a bundle of selfish needs and desires. They emanate from what Freud called the *id* i.e. from the amoral instinctual self which is orientated toward the immediate, here and now satisfaction of its desire for pleasure. Naturally enough, parents try to socialise their very young children by trying to integrate them into the life of the home without causing too much disruption. Because the child has no internal sense of conscience, the parents have to act as external arbiters of what is right and wrong. They do this by setting standards and by letting the child know what they expect. While they can use rewards and punishments in order to get a willful child to comply with their expectations, it isn't always easy or successful. However the parents have one powerful sanction at their disposal. In the last analysis, the child needs their love more than it needs to do its selfish thing. So if the parents threaten to withdraw their love when the child does something wrong, it will usually be willing to conform to their expectations in order to retain their approval and affection. The dynamic involved goes something like this.

The Experience of Conditional Love

In the course of being disciplined, a child can get the impression that the love of its parents is conditional. It depends on its willingness to tow the line and to do as it is told. This message is conveyed in non verbal ways. Facial appearance, tone of voice and body language seem to say to the baby, 'I will love you more if, ... if you don't cry ... if you don't get into a temper tantrum ... if you do as you are told etc.' Verbally parents can say such things as 'If you do such and such, mummy won't talk to you ... You are a bad boy ... a bad girl for doing that ... etc.' If the child feels that one or other of its parents is withdrawing its love on account of some wrong doing, it comes to the emotional rather than the rational conclusion that it must be a *bad person* to do such a bad thing. As such it is unlovable. This impression is often associated with feelings of abandonment, isolation, guilt and separation anxiety. As Freud wrote, 'Consciousness of guilt was originally fear of punishment by parents; more exactly, fear of losing their love.'[67] Not surprisingly therefore, the child desires to end its distress by appeasing its parents as a result of conforming to their expectations. It is important to point out that pre-rational emotional attitudes like these can influence people for the rest of their lives.

As the child grows, it develops what Freud referred to as an ego. It is the rational, executive aspect of the personality, which is in touch with reality and capable of developing an internal as opposed to an external sense of right and wrong. It expresses itself in the language of personal conviction such as, 'I want ... I desire ... I believe ... I need etc' However at the same time the child forms a superego. It internalises the moral attitudes of its parents and society in the form of conscience. As such it is a principle of pre-personal censorship and control, that makes itself felt in the form of abstract do's and dont's. Freud explains, 'This new psychical agency (i.e. a power of the mind) continues to carry on the functions which have hitherto been performed by the people in the external world: it observes the ego, gives it orders, judges it and threatens it with punishments, exactly like the parents whose place it has taken.'[68] The superego expresses itself in the impersonal language of obligation e.g. 'I must, I have to, I should, I ought etc.' As someone has observed, the language of conviction belongs to ourselves, the language of obligation belongs to others. The former fosters inner freedom while the latter can lead to a servile and legalistic conformism.

So, in the Freudian view, the personality consists of an interplay of three aspects, id, ego, and superego. The ego as the responsible executive aspect of personality, has to arbitrate between the conflicting demands of the id and the superego. It is worth pointing out that one can distinguish between a healthy and an unhealthy superego. The former represents the inherited values of a society or culture,[69] the latter does the same thing but in an arbitrary, tyrannical way, that demands unquestioning obedience and compliance. Failure to do so, means that it withdraws love and approval from the personality, in a punitive way that evokes a sense of remorse and separation anxiety.

Not surprisingly, a child may feel angry with its parents either for failing to satisfy its desires, or for abusing it in some way or other e.g. sexually, or by means of severe physical punishments. Either way, the child feels afraid of expressing its negative emotions lest it might evoke the disapproval of the parents. As a result, the feelings of resentment and even rage are turned inwards. They attack the child and tend to turn into feelings of insecurity and inferiority. Once the child gets used to this dynamic, it becomes second nature, so that in adult life it often converts repressed anger into feelings of anxiety and even depression. This is an important point. I believe that a good deal of adult anxiety, is in fact a form of repressed and unresolved anger.

The Superego and Negative Images of God

The psychology of religion has pointed to the fact that just as our positive God images are formed in childhood as a result of positive experiences of parental love, so negative images are formed as a result of a deprivation of such love. As people relate to their unhealthy superegos so they tend to relate to the Lord. At the conscious level of course, they may have positive concepts of God as loving, merciful, understanding, gentle, compassionate etc. But these are constantly challenged and undermined at an unconscious level by contradictory impressions and feelings. God's love is conditional says the superego. It is based on one's ability to live up to the demands of the law. Failure to do so results in a withdrawal of divine love, the threat of condemnation and punishment, together with an interior sense of morbid guilt and a numbing sense of alienation and anxiety. As Gregory Baum has written; 'The image of God the punisher has flourished in the Christian and even post-Christian imagination and is drawn from personal pathology. The idea of God as a judge on a throne, meeting out punishment, corresponds to the self-destructive trend of the human psyche.' He goes on to add, 'The person who is dominated by his superego – and no one can escape it altogether – has the accuser, judge, and tormentor all wrapt up in one, built into his own psychic makeup.' [70]

It is worth noting at this point, that just as we can repress feelings of anger which have been evoked by our parents so we can repress similar feelings which have been evoked by the Lord for one reason or another e.g. because the Almighty failed to answer our prayers on behalf of a dying relative.[71] Repressed emotions of this kind can also turn to anxiety. It follows therefore, that if we admit and express our repressed sense of hurt and anger, our feelings of anxiety will diminish. Finally, it would seem that the neurotic fear of guilt and condemnation we have been examining, is related to the second of the typical forms of ontological anxiety described by Tillich.

Separation Anxiety in Adult life

Happiness in adult life can be undermined by a tendency to anxiety which may be genetically inherited. It can also be adversely affected by separation anxiety of a neurotic kind. People who suffer from this type of fear in childhood, i.e. about 20% of the population,[72] often complain in adult life that other people are reluctant to get as close to them as they would like. They fear that their partners don't really love them and suspect that they will not stay with them. Their fear of abandonment is mixed with a yearning to merge completely with the other person. But this suffocating desire sometimes scares other people away, thereby confirming the lover's worst fears and plunging him or her into separation anxiety. Insecure people, have an exaggerated need to be accepted, liked and approved. As a result they tend to suppress a lot of their needs, thoughts and feelings in an overweening desire to please other people and to win and retain their esteem, affection and respect. But as Dorothy Rowe has observed, 'Tragically, most of us were taught as children that we were not good enough. We grew up not valuing ourselves, and thus are for ever giving to other people the power to *annihilate us* (my italics).'[73] It is that fear of being annihilated that terrifies us. Without the love and approval of others we could cease to exist as persons. But it is unrealistic to expect that everyone will like us all the time. Indeed it is unlikely that even our nearest and dearest will invariably do so. The fact is, as persons and as children of God, we have intrinsic value, and as such are worthy of love no matter what other people think.

The Superego, Guilt and Temptation

When people like these also suffer from unhealthy superegos their troubles are doubled. Usually, they are idealistic and perfectionistic. As such, they are subject to an exaggerated fear of failure, especially when they cannot fulfil their moral duties e.g. those of a sexual nature. If perchance they are unable, either because of weakness or even malice, to live up to their own high moral standards, they suffer a double loss. Like their own superegos, they suspect that God withdraws his love and approval from their personalities. As a result they feel condemned, cut off, and filled with a sense of shame and anxiety. They feel sorry not because they have failed to love God, but because they fear that he no longer loves them. In order to lessen their separation anxiety they sometimes experience a strong need to appease the God of conditional love by making a so called 'good confession'.

If they go to the sacrament of reconciliation, they examine their consciences in a moralistic and impersonal way, instead of inviting the Lord who searches everyone, to enlighten their hearts to know their sins and to enable them to trust in his mercy. In practice, they look at their relationship with God from the point of view of their shortcomings rather than looking at their shortcomings from the point of view of their relationship with God. They also worry about the way in which they confess their sins e.g. have they told the priest as a suitable authority figure, the kind of sins they have committed and how often? The superego says what they *should* do so, but a sense of shame tends to hold them back. Their preoccupation with the integrity of their confession means that they end up by investing more trust in the way in which they ought to confess than they do in the mercy and love of God. When they receive absolution they feel relief rather than peace. As long as the superego and its associated negative God images predominate, there is neither growth in relationship with themselves or with the Lord. Consequently, despite their firm purposes of amendment, they often find they have the desire but not the power to avoid sin in the future. So when they fail again, they return to the psycho-spiritual tread-mill where anxiety often leads to sin, and where sin in turn reinforces the underlying anxiety thereby completing the vicious circle of neurotic anguish and guilt.

Sexual Problems and the Superego

Despite their ethical ideals, people who are burdened with unhealthy superegos tend to suffer from two interrelated problems. Firstly, because they are, by and large, strangers to unconditional love, they find it hard to refrain from judging and condemning others in thought and word. One can take it for granted that they are treating their neighbours in the harsh moralistic way that they already treat themselves. Not surprisingly, this negative attitude of mind tends to alienate people from the men and women it hurts, thereby robbing them of the very love that they secretly crave. Secondly, an overbearing and punitive superego tends to weaken the confidence and authority of the ego. As a result the personality feels disconnected and out of touch with the meanings that enliven it. Free floating anxiety and mild depression begin to gain the upper hand. The unconscious Id tries to compensate, by prompting desires for comfort and pleasure.

Not surprisingly many of these desires are sexual in nature. The fact that so many of them seem to arise without any external stimulus, is an indication that they are rooted not in conscious lust, but rather in anxiety of a largely unconscious kind. Joyce Ridick a psychologist who works in the Gregorian University in Rome, has stated that up to 80% of our sexual impulses are 'a manifestation of unintegrated non-sexual needs which underlie the sexual symbolisation ... For example, when a need for dependency is not gratified, the person may, in anger and fear, seek gratification from themselves.'[74] Frank Lake makes much the same point in his book on *Clinical Theology*.[75] When a person with an unhealthy superego engages in erotic acts or fantasies that offend against conscience, temporary relief can be followed by a sense of anxiety that is reinforced by a self-absorbed form of guilt. And so a vicious circle is created, one that can lead to a great deal of unhappiness. As one writer has observed, 'We can pay rent to the superego but the house never becomes our own possession.' [76]

Overcoming separation anxiety

We have already noted in chapters four and five how separation anxiety is rooted in anxiety of an ontological kind. So having acknowledged the presence of neurotic anxiety and its immediate causes in our personal lives, it is important to go a step further by acknowledging that it is ultimately rooted in the objective threat of non-being. Then we can try to resolve it in one or other of the ways we have already described. That said, however, there are a number of things we can do in order to lessen separation anxiety as such. Firstly, in prayer we can contemplate the unconditional love of Him who said, 'Can a woman forget her nursing child, or show no compassion for the child of her womb? Even these may forget, yet I will not forget you.' Is 49:15.

Focusing on the Uncoditional Love of God

Having acknowledged that 'God is love' 1 Jn 4:16, you can hear Jesus say to your heart, 'As the Father loved me, so I love you' Jn 15:9. Then we can go on in the words of Paul to pray that, 'You may have your roots and foundation in love, so that you, together with all God's people may have the power to understand how broad and long, how high and deep, is Christ's love. Yes, may you come to know his love – although it can never be fully known – and so completely filled with the very nature of God' Eph 2:18. Then *imagine* that Jesus is kneeling before you with a towel wrapped around his waist. *Notice* that he is looking at you with eyes filled with *love* and *humility*. He is not there to tell you what he wants, rather he wants to know what you want from him as you pay attention to his love.

As I did this on one occasion I heard the Lord say these words to my heart. Perhaps they will bless you as they blessed me. 'I do not despise your imperfection. I live in it. When you see the flaws in your brothers and sisters, and the wounds of your own heart, do not feel that they will separate you from me. I live in those wounds. I reveal myself through your brokenness. When you look at the cross you do not see a perfect Lord, but a broken one. You do not see light but darkness. You do not see joy, but anguish and pain. My child, I have descended into the depths of your imperfection, there to reveal the glory of my Father. For I love you in your brokenness and you run away from it, as if it were not acceptable to me, as if I would despise it. It is my treasure. My light shines forth in all that you fear. So look to it. Accept it, in the knowledge that I am within it, and you will learn to see me in places you have never seen me before and in a world that frightens you today. You will see my face shining through tomorrow, for you will have changed, you will see as I see. My Glory is everywhere.'

Healing of Memories

Secondly, having acknowledged how we were hurt in the past, especially in childhood, we can bring our needs to the Lord in the eucharist, in order to be healed in mind and thereby protected from all anxiety, much as we describe in chapter 12 below. If we know a person with a healing ministry, we could also ask him or her to pray for healing of memories. Thirdly, we can also experience healing by progressively revealing our deepest thoughts, feelings, hurts and desires to a trusted friend or confidant. Research has confirmed the truth of Erikson's belief, that no matter how hurt we may have been in childhood, the experience of loving intimacy in adult life can progressively heal us in such a way that separation anxiety lessens bit by bit. Although anxious people tend to be mistrustful in relationships, the desire to love and be loved can give us the power to go courageously beyond the limitations which are normally set by fear to engage in honest self-disclosure. Then as we experience the understanding, acceptance and love of our friend, counsellor, or spouse, we begin to understand, accept and love our true selves in a new way. As we become more secure, as a result of this dynamic, we begin to trust people and indeed all of reality in such a way that anxiety gives way to joy as our deepest response to the mystery of being.

From Obligations to Convictions

If we suffer from unhealthy superego anxiety we can do a number of things. Firstly, it is good to acknowledge that there is a real difference between an unhealthy and a mature conscience. The prohibitions of the former do not arise as a result of appreciating the intrinsic goodness or badness of an action, whereas the latter is able to do so in terms of its relationship to Christ and his values. Secondly, try to become aware of the superego's activity in two ways, by noticing how often you use the language of obligation, and by becoming aware of characteristic, tell-tale feelings of isolation and remorse, whenever you fail to do your duty. Thirdly, when you are faced with a moral decision, instead of asking the question, 'In the light of what the law requires of me, what *ought* I do in these circumstances?' ask instead, 'In the light of my relationship with God and my own personal values, what do I *want* to do in these circumstances?' This is a vital question for all those who want to enjoy the freedom of the children of God.

I can recall an occasion when I was doing the prayer exercise mentioned in the previous section. I was noticing that Jesus was looking at me with love and *humility*. I said to him, 'Why be humble before me, when it is I who should be humble before you?' Then I suddenly realised that Jesus comes to us as one who serves. He doesn't come to us, as I had thought heretofore, like a latter day Moses armed with intimidating commandments carved on tablets of stone. He is not demanding, insisting in an authoritarian way, that we do what he wants, or else! Rather, in his love he reverences and respects our dignity and freedom, by asking what it is that we want, in the belief that it is the Spirit of his Father that prompts such holy desires within us. (cf Phil 2:13) We begin by concentrating on what he can do for us, e.g. by giving us an interior sense of his forgiveness and love. Then we move on to concentrate on what we can do for him. The Spirit prompts us to say, 'Lord I want only what you want.' It is at this stage of the Christian life, then that we not only appreciate the meaning of the beatitudes, we also find that we have both the desire and the power to apply them in our daily lives. We do this, not as a means of winning God's love, but rather as the grateful expression of the unconditional love we have already received.

Focusing on the Mercy of God

Fourthly, whenever we suspect that we are the victims of unhealthy superego guilt, we can focus our attention on the unconditional mercy of God. Although we have mentioned this subject in other chapters, we can add a new dimension in this one. I have found that three gospel stories are particularly helpful in couteracting superego problems. In the parable of the prodigal in Lk 15:12-32, the younger son represents the Id. He breaks away from the authority of his father and of the Jewish faith, in order to lead a self-indulgent life devoted to wine, women and song. The elder brother represents the moralistic superego in so far as he is a man of duty who is judgemental, resentful, and vindictive, and who relates to his brother and father in a legalistic way devoid of love. The father in the story represents the ego when it is touched by God's grace. It is loving and compassionate. Like the father it is willing to forgive the excesses of the Id and to respect but not to go along with the legalistic attitudes of the superego.

The story of the woman who came to the house of Simon the Pharisee in order to wash the feet of Jesus, Lk 7:36-50, is much the same. Mary the prostitute, the woman of lust and greed, rep-

resents the Id. Because of his self-righteous and judgemental attitude, Simon represents the overbearing superego. Jesus represents the Christian ego, and its un self-conscious, understanding,
and loving attitudes. Finally, the story of the pharisee and the tax
collector in Lk 18:9-15, is similar. The pharisee represents the
superego. He is proud, self-satisfied, and judgemental. In contrast
the tax collector is not only immoral and dishonest, he is also dis-
loyal to his people. As such he represents the Id. In his comments
Jesus reflects the attitudes of the Christian ego. In all three stories,
it is striking that although the characters representing the Id and
the superego are separated from God by their impersonal attitudes, Jesus indicates that because it is humiliated by its excesses,
the Id is more likely to desire closer union with God, than the self-
righteous superego which is often unaware of its lack of love. As
St Peter observed, 'God opposes the proud but accords his favour
to the humble' 1 Pt 5:5.

The superego and Confession

When Catholics are convinced that they are struggling
with superego problems they would be well advised to avoid the
unhelpful approach to confession described above. I have found
that the following points are helpful. Penitents need to begin by
focusing on the Lord and his love. Then they ask the Holy Spirit to
enlighten them by allowing them to see how they have failed to
respond to the love that God has shown them. If they wish to use
a written examination of conscience, it is not safe to do so unless it
is conducted within the prayerful context just described. Due to
the fact that the superego tends to centre its attention on righting
past wrongs, seen as atomised units, the penitent should look not
just at sinful acts, but at things such as worldly values, unacknowledged feelings of a negative kind and the neurotic attitudes
which may be influencing them.

As a priest I have discovered that many people with superego problems are like compulsive hand washers, they keep coming to confession in an anxious effort to be cleansed and to get
back into God's good books. That being so, I advise such people to
come to confession at predetermined intervals every eight weeks
or so, instead of running to the sacrament every time they are

troubled by neurotic guilt. Unless they are morally certain that they have committed grave sin, which is fairly unlikely in well intentioned people, they should give themselves the benefit of the doubt, make a sincere act of sorrow and continue receiving communion until the time of their next confession when it would be appropriate to mention anything that is troubling them. I have found that instead of leading to lax consciences, this approach weakens the malign influence of the superego, increases inner freedom and encourages spiritual growth.

Phobias

In this section we will be looking at phobic disorders. Like separation anxiety they are rooted in ontological anxiety. But they differ from free floating anxiety, which is afraid of everything in general and nothing in particular, in that they focus on particular threats for a short period of time. Phobic disorders are persistent, irrational fears of objects e.g. spiders, or situations e.g. heights. Apparently they afflict about 4% of the general population. We will look at three in particular, agoraphobia, social phobia and simple phobias.

Agoraphobia

Imagine you are in a familiar place like the local supermarket. Although you have been there many times before, this is an occasion like no other. Suddenly, and unexpectedly terror suddenly overwhelms you. Your heart pounds, you can't get enough air, you break into a sweat, your mind races, you are filled with a sense of inner chaos. You feel that you have to escape. This is what a panic attack is like. It is also the source of a fairly common but severe form of phobia called agoraphobia. The word itself comes from Greek meaning, 'fear of the market place'. Specifically it is a fear of all kinds of open spaces, especially when the afflicted person is unaccompanied by anyone else. Sufferers, who are about 1% of the population are twice as likely to be female than male. They may be people who have experienced severe reactions to separations in childhood. So in adult life they are inclined to play it safe by staying indoors as much as possible. An American psychiatrist called Donald Klein has discovered that victims of agoraphobia have often experienced panic attacks in the past.[77] Indeed, he suggests that their fear of going outdoors may be focused on the possibility of having to endure such a panic attack while away from home.

Social and Simple Phobias

People who suffer from this phobia are afraid that they will be humiliated or embarrassed in public place e.g. eating in a cafe or speaking at a meeting. It tends to afflict people in their twenties who are shy and solitary by nature. As their name implies, simple phobias are the most common. They involve fears of particular objects or situations. In the Reader's Digest Reverse Dictionary, there is a list of 73 different phobias. Some are common, such as acrophobia, the fear of heights; astraphobia, the fear of lightening; and arachnaphobia, the fear of spiders etc. Many others are less common such as dorophobia, the fear of fur; phasmophobia, the fear of ghosts; and triskaidekaphobia, the fear of the number thirteen.

Overcoming Phobic Reactions

In my experience phobias are not easy to control or to cure. Experts have tried different methods such as flooding, i.e. exposing people to the objects or situations that they fear the most. 'The patient is helped to break the phobic cycle by having him make a deliberate effort to feel and to experience fully this fear without trying to escape from it.'[78] The theory maintains that the initial state of intense anxiety is followed by a collapse of the symptoms. Not only that, the sufferer overcomes his or her fear of fear, which may be a key element in the phobia. The results seem to be quite good especially for simple and social phobias. With patience and the help of an encouraging therapist, many people can overcome their avoidance and get used to spiders, eating in public, etc.

Desensitisation is the name of another therapeutic method.[79] Firstly the phobic person does a relaxation exercise, then he or she is asked to imagine a mildly fearful version of their phobia. When they get used to that, they imagine more frightening situations and so on. The theory behind this treatment maintains that once the phobic person can tolerate the imagined object or situation without too much anxiety, he or she will be able to do the same in reality. Apparently it works fairly well in cases of minor phobia.

People can also be helped to cope with phobic disorders by availing of psychotherapy. While it may uncover the underlying causes of the fear, unfortunately it is not very effective at overcoming it. When anxiety is particularly acute, tranquillisers and even anti-depressants can be used for a short time to control the worst symptoms. It is possible that the most painful aspects of panic attacks can be controlled by deep breathing exercises, because apparently people in such states of distress tend to hyperventilate in a way that reinforces the problem.

Viktor Frankl proposed a third form of therapy called 'Paradoxical Intention'.[80] It argues that people can overcome their anticipatory fear of blushing, fainting etc. by good humoredly reversing their intention. For example, when I was teaching in a secondary school, class could be disrupted by a pupil who was hiccupping in a loud and uncontrolable way. The attention of classmates would focus on the person with the problem. Some would joke, others would slap him on the back, while others would ply him with good advice. On a number of occasions I overcame the problem by trying to reverse the victim's intention. I would take out all the money I had in my pocket, put it on the desk in front of me and say, 'hiccup one more time and you can take every penny!' The hiccupper would look at me and the money with utter surprise, he would try to hiccup, urged on of course by the other pupils, but all to no avail. No one ever got the money. Theoretically the same technique could be applied to phobias. In other words people would overcome their fear of lightening by intending to be more frightened by it than ever before, during the next electrical storm. In practice however, this approach doesn't work very well. Who would really want to be more afraid then ever before?

Conclusion

The subject of neurotic anxiety is a large and complex one. We have overlooked many aspects such as stress and burnout,[81] compulsive obsessions e.g. fear of doing violent deeds, and post-traumatic stress disorders. Helpful books are available in the larger bookshops which deal with problems like these. There are also self help groups such as 'Grow' which aim to assist people with emotional disorders. They use a philosophy and methodology which owes a lot to Alcoholics Anonymous. They suggest that a person suffering from an emotional upset can learn to cope better by asking the following four questions.

1. Be Definite.
Answer the question:
What exactly am I troubled about?
2. Be Rational.
Answer the question:
Is it certain, probable or only possible?
3. Be Wise.
Answer the question:
How important is it?
4. Be Practical.
Answer the question:
What shall I do about it?

Grow groups also use an adapted version of the twelve steps which include the following important points.
- We admitted that we were inadequate or maladjusted to life.
- We surrendered to the healing power of God.
- We learned to think by reason rather than by feelings and imagination.
- We trained our wills to govern our feelings.

Finally, they say the following prayer for maturity:
'True, strong and loving God, teach me to see things as they really are, to accept myself and to trust fearlessly in your care, to govern myself, and to find my peace in doing your will, and living or dying to give myself back to You.'

CHAPTER 7

Courageous Faith Expressed in Praise

We have seen how we can be threatened by all kinds of fearful problems. I have noticed that there is often a temptation to wrestle with difficulties, instead of nestling in the Lord, to magnify problems, instead of magnifying Him who has overcome them all. He said, 'In this world you will have trouble. But take heart! I have overcome the world' Jn 16:33. At the end of this section, we will take a look at one biblical way of expressing confidence in the victory of the Lord. In Hebrew it is called the *teruwah* or shout of praise.[82] It is voiced by those who affirm and anticipate the delivering power of God, in the face of seemingly impossible odds and situations. In the Bible there are three forms of anticipatory praise, messianic, paschal, and eschatological. The first has to do with the Old Testament period, the second with the ministry of Jesus and the third with the present time which precedes the second coming of the Lord. We will look at each type in turn.

Messianic Praise

In the Old Testament there are frequent references to Jewish military history. Over and over again, the people of God had to face armies that were larger and better equipped than their own. But they had a secret weapon so to speak. They had a confidence that God would be fighting with them. No matter what the odds against them, victory would be theirs. There is an example of this in Ex 14:14. The Jewish people were faced by the might of the Egyptian army. But God said, 'Do not be afraid. Stand firm and you will see the deliverance the Lord will bring you today ... The Lord will fight for you; you need only be still.' Because Jewish soldiers had this assurance from the Lord, their battle cries had a liturgical ring. They began to chant the *teruwah* as they marched to war. It was a piercing cry, one that was meant to strike terror into their enemies, and to anticipate the victory that God would give them.

This was the case at Jericho. It was a walled city that seemed to be impregnable from a military point of view. But the Lord said to Joshua the Jewish leader, 'See I *have* (my italics, the deed is already accomplished in principle) delivered Jericho into your hands' Jos 6:2. He went on to say that the priests and people were to march round the city for six days. On the seventh, the priests were to blow the trumpets of praise, 'When you hear them sound a long blast, have all the people give a loud shout; then the wall of the city will collapse' Jos 6:5. Anticipating the fulfilment of God's promises, the people shouted the teruwah to God. The walls fell, the city was taken, victory was theirs, 'Not by might nor by power, but by my Spirit,' will victory be accomplished, 'says the Lord Almighty' Zech 4:6.

What applied on the battlefield was also true in the lives of individuals when faced by the intimidating challenges of everyday life. There are two examples that have inspired me for years. Firstly, there is the mythical case of the three young men who despite the threats of King Nebuchadnezzer refused to worship false gods. Although they were faced with the terrifying prospect of being thrown into a fiery furnace they proclaimed, 'If our God whom we serve is able to deliver us from the furnace of blazing fire and out of your hand, O king, let him deliver us. *But if not ,* (my italics) let it be known to you, O king, that we will not serve your gods.' Dan 3:17-18. It is worth noting that the commitment of the young men was unconditional. They knew that God could deliver them, but their faithfulness did not depend upon his doing so. When they were thrown into the flames, instead of panicking, the trio expressed their unshakeable faith by shouting out their *teruwah* Dan 3:24-91. It proved to be the prelude to their remarkable liberation. Suddenly, someone like a child of the gods was seen among them. The king was so impressed that he said, 'Shadrach, Meshach and Abed-Nego, servants of God Most High, come out, come here!' Dan 3:93. And so the young men were set free.

The mythical story of Jonah is similar. He faced the dreadful prospect of being thrown into the sea and swallowed by a whale. It must have been a horrifying experience to be entombed in the dark dank interior of this giant creature of the sea. Instead of being frozen with fear and despair, the prophet cried out his *teruwah* of praise, 'Some abandon their faithful love,' he cried, 'by worshipping false gods, but I shall sacrifice to you with songs of praise. The vow I have made I shall fulfil! Salvation comes from Yahweh!' Although he had no hope of deliverance from a human point of view, his outburst of unconditional praise was followed by liberation, 'Yahweh spoke to the fish,' we are told, 'which then vomited Jonah onto the dry land.' Jon 2:9-11.

Later in the Old Testament we find that when the chosen people settled down in Palestine there were fewer wars and dangers than heretofore. But they remembered the battle cry of victory. They modified it for use in their temple worship. It became the 'festal shout'. It is mentioned in the psalms. For example in Ps 47:1-6 we read, 'Clap your hands, all you nations; shout to God with cries of joy....God has ascended amid shouts of joy, the Lord amid the sounding of trumpets.' Ps 89:15 sums up the biblical attitude, 'Blessed are the people who know the festal shout.' As the people anticipated the manifestation of the victory and power of God in their own lives, they were also anticipating the coming of the Messiah. He would inaugurate the final and definitive victory of God. Their messianic praise anticipated the coming of Jesus and his proclamation of the advent of the kingdom of God.

Paschal Praise

Expectancy gave way to fulfilment in the life and ministry of Jesus Christ. It came to its climax on Palm Sunday. The people greeted Jesus as the Messiah. Their hopes were pinned on him in the belief that he would take possession of Jerusalem, drive out the Romans and establish the reign of God. So they waved palms, shouted praises and chanted lines from Ps 117 'Hosanna to the Son of David! Blessed is he who comes in the name of the Lord! Hosanna in the highest' Mt 21:9. We think of the word 'hosanna' as a cry of praise. In Hebrew it literally means 'save us.' But the Jews had such confidence that their prayer would be answered that it became a cry of praise that anticipated the impending victory of God. When some Pharisees in the crowd said to him, 'Master check your disciples,' Jesus replied, 'I tell you, if these keep silence, the stones *will cry out*' Lk 19:40. In other words Jesus realised that the praise of the people was prophetic in a way they didn't understand. Their *teruwah* anticipated the defeat not of the Romans, but of Satan, sin, and death in the victory of the resurrection.

There is reason to believe that Jesus echoed the people's festal shout as he died on the cross, Betrayed, denied and deserted, he even felt abandoned by God, and quoted the opening line of Ps 22, 'My God, My God why have you forsaken me?' In his book on the psalms, Albert Gelin comments, 'This complaint is not that of a rebel or of someone in despair. It is that of a just man, suffering and yet assured of the love and protection of the all-holy God which will accompany him even to death ... The cry is not, in the Jewish sense, an expression of despair; it does not express a revolt, but remains in harmony with the devotion of the Old Testament and, in consequence, expresses a sense of communion with God.'[83] Gelin also points out that if a Jew quoted the first line of a prayer, book or document, he or she was evoking it in its entirety. This would lead us to believe that Jesus silently recalled the rest of of Ps 22. Having expressed his sense of anguish we have reason to believe that he identified with the following words, 'I will tell of your name to my brothers and sisters; in the midst of the congregation I will praise you: You who fear the Lord, praise him! ... Future generations will be told about the Lord and proclaim his deliverance to a people yet unborn, saying that he has done it.' Jesus never lost faith in his Father's power to save. As the end came, he affirmed this. '*He cried out in a loud voice*, Father into your hands I commend my spirit' Lk 23:46. This is the victorious *teruwah* of Christ, his Paschal praise, that anticipates his resurrection from the dead.

Eschatological Praise

We live in the last phase of history. The power of Satan, sin and death, have been broken in principle by the death and resurrection of Jesus. They will be finally and completely defeated when Christ returns in glory. No wonder the commonest cry of the early church was *Maranatha*! i.e. 'Come Lord Jesus.' Like the cry of 'hosanna,' it was a prayer of petition which was uttered with such confidence, that it became transformed into a prayer of praise. This festal shout of the first Christians, their eschatological praise, anticipated the final and definitive victory of God in history.

It is my belief that the Lord is calling us to echo the festal praise of New Testament times. There are a number of reasons for doing this. Firstly, as Christians we have formidable problems to face in our own lives, in the Church and in society. As a result, many people suffer. Their suffering will make them bitter not better if they lose confidence in the presence, power and promises of the Lord. Secondly, it would be naive to think that the obstacles we face are only human. As I point out in other chapters, ultimately 'Our struggle is not with flesh and blood, but against ... the spiritual forces of evil in the heavenly realms' Eph 6:12. But as we cry our praises to the Lord who delivers us from all evil, the power of Satan is overcome.[84] Thirdly, anticipatory praise opens the heart to experience the revelation of the Lord. As Ps 22:3 puts it, 'God lives in the praises of his people!' Perhaps Jesus was comforted when he recalled this biblical promise on the cross. In the midst of our sufferings we can do the same by uttering prayers of confident praise. As the fourth weekday preface puts it, 'God has no need of our praise, yet our desire to praise him is itself his gift. Our praise adds nothing to his greatness, but helps us grow in his grace.'

Praise the Short Cut to Freedom

My conviction about the importance and power of praise was nurtured in the North of Ireland. Because we faced impossible odds, we had to rely on God. For example, an ecumenical conference took place during the general strike of May 1977. It was a time of great unrest and fear. There was violence in the streets and the threat of power failures. The organising committee feared that many people would have to cancel their registrations. They didn't. Over a thousand Protestants and Catholics met in Church House in the centre of Belfast for a 'Festival of Praise.' It was a remarkable experience. There was an outburst of praise, of festal shouts of joy, such as I had never heard before. As we glorified the Lord we knew that he who was in us was greater than all the things we had reason to fear in the world. In a prophecy, the Lord called upon us to be united as his army. 'The work and the weapons are one,' he said, 'They are praise.' Those words are as relevant today as they were back in the seventies.

We are living through a time of tribulation and purification. We have many fearful problems to face, the breakdown of traditional values, the increasing crime rate, not to mention our own personal and family worries. We can mourn and weep that the body of Christ is broken. But we have to be careful not to grieve in a worldly manner that leads to hopelessness and depression. Rather we grieve in that Godly fashion that leads to a change of heart. (cf 2 Cor 7:10). As we do, 'God will comfort us in all our afflictions' 2 Cor 1:4. In this way, the Lord fulfils the promise in the Beatitudes which says, 'Blessed are they who mourn, they shall be comforted' Mt 5:5. Knowing that this is so, we begin to 'jubilate'[85] i.e. to praise God with enthusiasm. We anticipate in our praises the blessings he will shower on his people in the immediate future. We anticipate too that time when he will come again upon the clouds of heaven. Then the heavenly host will blow the trumpets and utter a mighty *teruwah*, that will usher in the kingdom of God. On that day, there will be no cause for fear, 'There will be no more death or mourning or crying or pain, for the older order of things will have passed away' Rev 21:4.

PART 3

Faith and Deliverance from Evil

'If the Catholic Church clearly affirms the existence and influence of the Powers of Evil, her systematic theology nonetheless remains very guarded on this subject. If ever there was a domain that must be approached very soberly, as St Paul advises, this is surely the one.'

(Cardinal Suenens, *Renewal and the Powers of Darkness* p. 77.)

CHAPTER 8

Catholic Thought
on the Devil's Existence

In his book, *Catholicism Confronts Modernity*, Protestant theologian Langdon Gilkey has suggested that the present crisis in the Catholic Church is due to the 'dissolution of the understanding of the supernatural as the central religious category.'[1] There is a great deal of truth in what he says. Nowadays we tend to interpret religious beliefs in terms of immanence rather than transcendence. While this is probably a good and necessary thing in the circumstances of modern secular culture – where there is a growing emphasis on subjective experience rather than objective authority - there is a distinct danger that some of our traditional beliefs will be watered down or abandoned altogether. In this chapter I propose to look at a test case, namely, belief in the existence of a personal devil. I have a number of reasons for doing so.

Firstly, the devil's defeat at Calvary had an important role to play in the traditional depiction of the drama of salvation. For example, the apostle John wrote, 'The reason the Son of God appeared was to destroy the works of the devil' 1 Jn 3:8. Theology has maintained that although defeated by Christ, Satan continued to have power to tempt people to commit sin, deliberately and knowingly.[2] Christians also believe that anything that tends to self-destruction such as sickness and death invariably can and must be regarded as an expression of diabolic powers, even though their immediate causes are natural.[3] For example the author of the letter to the Hebrews wrote, 'Since the children, as he calls them, are flesh and blood, Jesus himself became like them and shared their human nature. He did this 'so that through his death he might destroy the Devil, who has the power of death, and in this way set free those who were slaves all their lives because of their fear of death' Heb 2:14.

Theology also taught that although he was defeated by Christ, Satan continued to have power to tempt people to appear as an angel of light. Under the guise of an apparent good, he could prompt disordered desires and lead a person of good faith to make wrong decisions. Hence the emphasis on discernment of spirits in ascetical theology down the ages. Furthermore, since New Testament times the Church has maintained that it is possible to be oppressed, or in very rare cases to be possessed by the devil in such a way that the victim would require either deliverance or solemn exorcism.

Secondly, while there appears to be clear evidence for belief in the existence of a personal devil both in scripture and tradition, some theologians argue that such beliefs have to be seen as myths, or stories that speak about the experience of evil in imaginative ways. When they are demythologised, belief in the devil and his demons is no longer credible. For example referring to the writings of a fellow theologian, Hans Kung asserts, 'Herbert Haag has rightly bade 'goodbye to personified evil and belief in the devil, both of which have done untold harm.'[4] As we shall see later, there are other scholars who argue that if the evil one exists, we know nothing about him. At best his existence is irrelevant. At worst it can lead to all kinds of pathological superstitions and cruelties[5] and to the excesses of fundamentalist Christians who put an exaggerated and unhealthy emphasis on possession and exorcism.[6]

Thirdly, many of those who deny that the devil exists see him as a projection of the negative and daimonic aspects of human experience. A few years ago I expressed sentiments of this kind in response to a film review of *The Exorcist*. I suppose I'm one of those young priests mentioned by Fr Forristal in the May issue of *The Furrow* who wouldn't 'care to commit themselves too firmly to the existence of a personal devil'. But I am firmly committed to the reality of possession described by St Paul in Rm 7:20. 'If I do what I don't want to do, this means that no longer am I the one who does it, instead it is sin that lives in me.' Isn't it true to say that rather than being something positive, sin or evil is the absence of our true Christian identity, for one reason or another? This sort of spiritual vacuum can lead to all sorts of psychosomatic disorders where people become the victims of compulsive behaviour, sometimes of a bizarre and sinister kind. 'Possession' in this sense has been well described by many contemporary psychiatrists. For example, in his book *Love and Will*, Rollo May makes this interesting observation in a chapter on the nature of the daimonic. 'Satan, or the devil, comes from the Greek word *diabolos*; 'diabolic' is the term in contemporary English. *Diabolos*, interestingly enough, literally means 'To tear apart' (*dia-bollein*).' In other words the devil may be a personified projection of the experience of alienation or sin.[7]

Encounters with Evil

Shortly after writing that magazine piece, a number of events led me to re-examine my position. The process began when I experienced the kind of spiritual awakening which is sometimes referred to as 'baptism in the Spirit.' The effects were paradoxical ... On the one hand I became intensely aware of the person of Jesus and of his great love for me. On the other I had a heightened sense both of my own inner darkness and the darkness in the world around me. Some time later I went to Germany on holidays and happened to visit the gas chambers in Dachau Concentration Camp. It was a traumatic experience. I was so overwhelmed by the enormity of the crime committed there, and by extension in the other camps, that I sensed as never before that there was a real force of evil which seemed to be more than the personification of human alienation and sin. When I got home I happened to meet an officially appointed exorcist. He told me about some of the troubled people who had been referred to him. In spite of having received the best of medical and psychiatric help they had not improved until they had been exorcised. Indeed I actually saw him perform such an exorcism. After a few blood curdling roars and screams an afflicted woman was not only delivered from spiritual oppression, she found that a tumour on her neck seemed to have been completely healed. I must say that the whole episode made a deep impression on me. A few years later I had to perform a simple as opposed to a solemn exorcism,[8] myself. It followed a two month long discernment process and happily proved effective. It confirmed my growing conviction that evil spirits do in fact exist..

For years now I have sensed that many of the conflicts that we are currently experiencing in the Christian community are manifestations of a particularly intense struggle between the Spirit of God and the 'prince of this world.' I can only agree with Pope Paul VI when he said 'It was believed that after the second Vatican Council there would be a day of sunshine in the history of the church. There came instead a day of clouds, storm and darkness, of search and uncertainty. This came through an adverse power; his name is the Devil.' So it wasn't surprising that the Holy Father said that one of the greatest needs of the Church today 'is defense from the evil which is called the devil.' He went on to add, 'This question of the devil and the influence he can exert on individuals and communities, whole societies or events is a very important chapter of Catholic doctrine which is given little attention today, though it should be studied again.'

Finally, in the more recent past I have become increasingly aware of the danger of reductionist tendencies which interpret religious doctrines such as belief in the existence of the devil, in purely psychological terms. P. C. Vitz has shown how unscientific and unchristian are the assumptions underpinning much of the psychological theory used.[11] Psychiatrist Gerald May has also warned against the danger of 'psychidolatry'. When religion and psychology come together he warns, there is a possibility that, 'instead of integration there is an absorption of religion into psychology'. [12]

Intentions and Methodology

In this section I intend to do a number of things. Firstly, I will outline and evaluate the teaching of the scriptures and the liturgy about the evil one. Secondly, I will look at Church teaching and the opinions of theologians concerning the existence or non-existence of Satan. Thirdly, because of the contemporary tendency to psychologise the evil spirit out of existence, I will examine and evaluate what Freud, Jung and contemporary psychiatrists have said about demonology. Fourthly, I will try to arrive at a modern understanding of the devil and evil spirits, one that takes into account the mythological nature of a good deal of the Christian teaching about them. To do so I will refer to the writings of well known scholars in the relevant disciplines. Finally I will draw attention to some of the theological implications that seem to flow from the evaluation. Two general points. Although sin committed with our knowledge and consent is the all important way in which the spirit of evil touches our lives, it will not be the main focus of this investigation. Instead it will concentrate on the ways in which evil can 'possess' us to a greater or lesser extent, sometimes without our conscious knowledge or consent. For convenience sake, I will refer to the devil in masculine terms throughout this scetion. Needless to say, as an immaterial spirit it is in reality, neither male or female.

Demonology in the Gospels

In the Old Testament belief in Satan's existence was not very important. On the few occasions that he was mentioned, he usually embodied a threat to God's world, whether as divine prosecutor or as destructive principle. In the The New Testament period there were two schools of thought. The predominant one accepted inter-testamental beliefs about Satan and his demons, many of which were borrowed from surrounding cultures. The Saducees on the other hand, represented an alternative point of view. They neither believed in the resurrection of the dead nor in the existence of spirits either good or evil. In God's providence, Jesus became man when such differing views were prevelant. The fact that in a general sense, he chose to accept the demonology of his time, rather than the opinions of the Saducees, is significant. As one document put it, 'To maintain today, that words of Jesus about Satan express only a teaching borrowed from his culture and are unimportant for the faith of other believers is evidently to show little understanding either of the Master's character or of his age.'[13]

We can take an incomplete and impressionistic look at the importance of demonology in the ministry of Jesus. Hans Kung says that there is no evidence that Jesus developed a doctrine of demons.[14] But it would also be true to say that he developed the existing doctrine, such as it was. Joachim Jeremias has pointed out[15] that whereas in contemporary Judaism demons were seen predominantly as unorganised individual beings, haphazardly inclined to physical, psychological and moral evil, Jesus had a unified view of individual and collective evil . He saw Satan, the devil, as 'Prince of this World,' (Jn 12:31) the ruler and commander,

(Lk 10:19) of an organised army of demons. (Mk 5:9) This is significant surely. Jesus considered himself to be engaged in a spiritual struggle with his arch-enemy, who together with his minions were intimately associated with the many evils which afflict the human race such as death, disease and sin of all kinds.

The Devil, Demons and Spirits

The scriptures use three principal words to describe the evil one and his followers, namely, devil, demons, and spirits. The English words 'devil' and 'diabolical' are derived from the Greek *diabolos*, meaning 'the accuser,' 'slanderer,' or 'the one who divides.' Although the devil is variously referred to as Beelzebub and Belial, his most common name is 'Satan.' The word is derived from the Hebrew *sathan*, meaning 'adversary.' In a way his role, as a powerful and perverse creature, is the opposite to the divine role of Jesus and the Holy Spirit who are described as our 'advocates.' In the gospels the devil is described as 'the evil one,' Mt 13:19 'the enemy,' Lk 10:19 'ruler of the world,' Jn 12:31 'a murderer' and 'a liar, Jn 8:44 etc.

The word 'demon' comes from the Greek *daimon* which literally means 'knowing one.' Such creatures have a number of characteristics. For example, they act under the authority of Satan, Rev 16:13, they can afflict people with disease, Lk 13:16, tempt them with unclean thoughts, Mt 10:1; Mk 5:2; Lk 8:27-29 and they can possess men, women and even children, Lk 8:28. When we count the number of texts which speak of the devil and his demons, they are surprisingly large in number. The four gospels also refer to the existence of unclean spirits or *pneuma to akatharton* in Greek. They seem to be disembodied, independent, non-physical beings on about the same level as human beings, and lower than angels and demons. Most of the ones mentioned in the scriptures are malicious and destructive. For example, there are as many as twenty one references to unclean spirits in the synoptic gospels and the Acts.

Jesus Confronts the Devil

Theologian Edward Schillebeeckx has written, 'In the New Testament, Jesus' saving activity is depicted as a fight against the demonic powers of evil.'[16] From the beginning of his public ministry the evangelists highlight this confrontation between Jesus and Satan. Having been anointed by the Holy Spirit in the Jordan, he was led by the same Spirit into the wilderness, there to meet with Satan. Having resisted the adversary's temptations in the power of God's word, Luke comments, that the devil 'departed from him until an opportune time!' Lk. 4:13. Surely this text contains a chilling intimation of the final and decisive confrontation which would take place during Passion Week. Jesus himself often spoke about Satan in his sermons and stories. For example, his first extended discourse in Mark, is a sequence of parables ex-plaining that his exorcisms are signs of his victory over the devil Mk. 3:23-30. The parable of the sower shows that Satan poses the principal threat to the reception and fruitfulness of God's word Mk. 4:15. On the important occasion when Jesus announced his intention of going to Jerusalem, Peter tried to dissuade him. But the Lord replied, 'get behind me Satan! You are a hindrance to me; for you are not on the side of God but of men.' Mt 16:22-23.

If Jesus saw the devil as his arch-rival, the demons were his agents. Through his gift of discernment he often acknowl-edged that these evil spirits had caused the physical and mental afflictions that he encountered in suffering people. As a result, ex-orcism played an important part in his ministry. In Mk. 5:1-20 we have a dramatic account of the way in which the Lord drove out a demon from the Geresene demoniac. When Jesus met sick people, he was able to discern whether the presenting symptoms were due to psycho-physical causes, or to the influence of demons. For example, we are told that on separate occasions, two deaf and dumb boys were brought to him. The evangelist informs us that one 'He took aside in private, away from the crowd, put his fin-gers into the man's ears and touched his tongue with spittle .... and he said to him, 'Ephphatha,' that is, 'Be opened.' And his ears were opened, and the ligament of his tongue was loosened and he spoke clearly' Mk 7:33-35. In the case of the second lad, Jesus said, 'Deaf and dumb *spirit* ... I command you: come out of him and never enter him again' Mk 9:25-26. Commenting on exorcisms of this kind Jesus said, 'Since it is by the Spirit of God that I cast out demons, know that the kingdom of God has come among you' Mt

12:28. Scripture scholars believe that this quotation is probably an authentic historical saying of the Lord. It expresses one of the most distinctive and characteristic emphases of his teaching about the inbreaking of the Kingdom of God. St Peter summed up this aspect of Christ's ministry when he declared to Cornelius and his household, you have heard 'how God anointed Jesus of Nazareth with the Holy Spirit and power; how he went about doing good and *healing all that were oppressed by the devil,* for God was with him' Acts 10:38.

Jesus authorised his disciples to exorcise in his name. In Mk 3:14 we read, 'And he appointed twelve, to be with him, and to be sent out to preach and have authority to cast out demons.' When the apostles returned from one of their missionary expeditions they reported their successes to their master. Jesus replied, 'I saw Satan fall like lightening from heaven' Lk 10:17. Rudolf Bultmann has agreed that, from a strictly historical point of view, this is another of the authentic sayings of Jesus. It joyfully acknowledges the definitive defeat of the devil. Finally, before his Ascension into heaven Jesus commissioned the apostles to preach the good news to the ends of the earth, saying, 'And these signs will accompany those who believe: in my name they will cast out demons,' Mk 16:17.

The evangelists and later the other New Testament writers made it clear that the passion, death and resurrection of Jesus marked the victorious climax of his on-going confrontation with Satan. On one occasion Jesus expressed his understanding of the meaning and purpose of his impending death. 'Now is the judgement of this world,' he declared, 'now shall the ruler of this world be cast out; and I, when I am lifted up from the earth will draw all people to myself' Jn 12:21. The confrontation between Jesus and the evil one became poignantly obvious during Passion Week. 'The devil' explained one of the evangelists, 'had already prompted Judas Iscariot, son of Simon to betray Jesus,' Jn 13:2. The Lord himself recognised that the 'the hour of darkness' Lk 22:53 was close at hand. When it came, it was symbolised by the solar eclipse that occured as Jesus hung in spiritual desolation upon the cross (cf Lk 23:45). He submitted to death in faithfulness to his Father's saving will. What appeared to be Satan's victory, was in fact the moment of his decisive defeat. This was manifested on

Easter Sunday, when God vindicated his divine Son by raising him triumphantly from the dead. St John had every reason to proclaim, 'Now ... the accuser of our brothers and sisters, who accuses them day and night before our God, has been hurled down' Rev 12:10.

Evaluation of the Gospel Texts

How should we evaluate these texts? Do they reflect the actual mind of Christ, or are they the constructs of the early Church? Was his belief in Satan and the demons misguided in nature? In his book on demonology, Henry Kelly, like many other scholars, employs a sceptical attitude in assessing the N.T. data. He maintains that 'There is no systematic demonology present ... A common factor behind the biblical motifs is the need to describe intelligibly the cause of obstacles to human happiness. But the explanations are invariably flavoured by notions inherited or borrowed from cultures alien to Judaism.'[17] To describe the motive and sources of Jesus' demonolgy, in this way, does nothing to invalidate it's content. An official Anglican report on the subject of exorcism, has stated, 'One cannot get away from the fact that the New Testament is teaching a personal origin for evil; it simply will not do to dismiss this language as metaphor.'[18] Catholic Scripture scholar John P Meier agrees. He says that like his cures, the exorcisms of Jesus were signs and partial realisations of the coming of the kingdom of God. Nevertheless, commentators like Kelly, try to explain away those very exorcisms in terms of psychological and cultural factors. 'Such a judgement' Meier rightly says, 'is based not on historical exegesis but on a *philosophical assumption about what God can and cannot do in this world* (my italics) - an assumption rarely if ever defended with rigorous logic. Instead, appeal is made to 'modern man,' who looks suspiciously like 18th-century Enlightenment man.'[19]

Theologian Louis Monden says in his influential book, *Signs and Wonders*, that to read the Scriptures with an open mind, without pre-conceived ideas, makes it clear that one cannot do away with the devil as a personal entity without changing the Christian message *in its very essence* [20] (My Italics). Victor White and Morton Kelsey both say something similar in their books, which are theological studies of the relationship between Jungian psychology and Christianity. They state that the words and actions of Jesus which are recorded in the gospels, epistles and especially the Apocalypse, are largely unintelligible unless one accepts the reality and activity of Satan and other malevolent spirits.[21] In an excellent Christological work, entitled *Jesus and the Spirit*, Protestant exegete James Dunn endorses this point when he notes that accounts of how Jesus healed mentally deranged and demon possessed people are historically accurate and reliable. Apparently exorcisms were the one group of miracles to which D.F. Strauss in his well known work on the mythical nature of the miracle stories in the gospels, attached a high degree of historical probability. There have been no developments in gospel criticism since then which have given any reason to question his judgement. On the contrary, they have reinforced the essential historicity and importance of Jesus' work as an exorcist. [22]

Demonology in the Pauline Writings

In his letters Paul talks about Satan on at least two occasions. In 2 Cor 11:14 he mentions that the devil can disguise himself as an angel of light. Writing about this in his *Spiritual Exercises*, St Ignatius pointed out that when a person is striving to lead a good life, the evil spirit, 'the enemy of our nature,' ordinarily manifests himself like an angel of light. He might use counterfeits of the supernatural kind such as 'visions,' 'revelations,' and 'prophecies' in order to mislead people. Indeed Ignatius recounts such a case in his Autobiography. He was deceived for a time by a vision of a beautiful creature with many eyes. Then one day, 'while kneeling before a cross, he saw clearly that the object did not have its usual beautiful colour, and with a strong affirmation of his will he knew very clearly that it was from the demon.'[23] The evil spirit can also inspire pious thoughts or holy desires which can eventually lead to intellectual pride and selfishness. For example, a person with business acumen might be inspired by his love of God to make lots of money in order to help others, only to be led bit by bit to such an all consuming drive for wealth as to become ruthless and unjust.

In 1 Cor 12:7 Paul recounts how he received a mysterious thorn in the flesh. We don't know what it was exactly, perhaps a disability like epilepsy, or a sexual inclination of a lustful kind. He says that it was a messenger of Satan the personification of pride, which paradoxically, prevented him from getting spiritually proud. In 2 Cor 10:3-6, St Paul writes, 'We live as human beings, but we do not wage our war according to human standards; for the weapons of our warfare are not merely human, but they have divine power to destroy strongholds. We destroy arguments and every proud obstacle raised up against the knowledge of God, and we take every thought captive to Christ.' This verse clearly employs the language of spiritual warfare. The true follower of the Lord can rely on divine power to expose and overcome the false thinking, attitudes and judgements of those who are not in right relationship with God and who may be under the influence of evil spirits.

Dominations, Principilaties and Authorities

The other epistles which are incorrectly attributed to Paul, assert that Christ is victorious over all 'dominations, principalities and authorities,' (cf Col 1:16; Eph 1:21) and the 'elements of the world' Col 2:20. Christians are encouraged to put on the whole armour of God because they 'are contending not with flesh and blood, but with principalities, powers, the world-rulers of the present darkness, the evil spiritual hosts' Eph 6:12. This perspective was probably influenced by the preaching of St Paul himself. Even if it was not, it forms an integral part of the inspired teaching of the New Testament Church. Stripped of its more bizarre mythological elements, this neo-Pauline perspective seems to refer, not so much to the devil himself, as to the structures and cultural mores he can sometimes use to dominate and condition our lives in the world. As Karl Rahner says, they are 'the powers of the world insofar as this world is a denial of God and a temptation to people'[24] They probably include things such as church structures, ideologies, codes, customs, elites, laws, economic arrangements and 'isms' of all kinds. The critiques of Marxists, Freudians, feminists and others have helped to uncover the oppressive nature of many aspects of the social status quo, which can have such an insidious but hidden effect upon our sense of self and values.

In his *Method and Theology*, theologian Bernard Lonergan

has described how individual and group egoism can lead to what different thinkers have called 'false consciousness.'[25] In spite of apparent economic, cultural and military succeses, it leads nations to increasing degrees of alienation and decline. He writes, 'A civilisation in decline digs its own grave with a relentless consistency. It cannot be argued out of its self destructive ways, for argument has a major theoretical premiss, theoretical premisses are asked to conform to matters of fact, and the facts in the situation produced by decline more and more are the absurdities that proceed from inattention, oversight, unreasonableness and irresponsibility.'[26] For example, Nietzsche and Scheler have shown how the values, attitudes and actions of individuals, groups and even societies can be motivated by what they call 'ressentiment.' This feeling of envious indignation is unconsciously evoked by the superior worth, talent, wealth, achievements or values of another person or group. Pilate recognised that it was this attitude that motivated the chief priests to demand the crucifixion of Jesus, 'he saw that it was out of envy he handed him over.' (cf Mk 15:10; & Wis. 2:12-24)

While they are not necessarily bad in themselves, secular and religious ideologies and institutions can hold sway over selfwilled people, 'you once followed the course of this world,' scripture says, 'following the ruler of the power of the air, the spirit that is now at work in the disobedient.' Eph 2:2. The ideologies and institutions already referred to, can even hold people in demonic servitude. For example, Gal 4:3 says, 'when we were children we were enslaved to the elemental spirits of the world,' and in Col 2:20-21 we read, 'If with Christ you died to the elemental spirits of the universe, why do you live as if you still belonged to the world? why do you submit to regulations, 'do not handle, Do not taste, do not touch'.'

That said, God still uses defective worldly organisations and urges people to subordinate themselves to them in all things that are not sinful. For example, Paul says in Rm 13:1, 'Let every person be subject to the governing authorities; for there is no authority except from God, and those authorities that exist have been instituted by God.' Ironically, the apostle to the gentiles can say this, in spite of the fact that he knows that it was those very authorities that crucified the Lord of Glory (cf 1 Cor 2:6-8) By doing so they ensured the downfall of the evil spirits that had acted through them. As Col 2:15 puts it, 'Having disarmed the powers and authorities, he made a public spectacle of them, triumphing over them by the cross.' It strikes me that this aspect of Paul's teaching is obscure. Whether it is relevant nowadays is debatable, other than to say that Jesus is Lord over any spirits, good and bad alike, who might try to influence us through worldly structures and authorities whether those of the state, church or family.

Demonology in the Liturgy

Patristic scholarship has shown how the early Christians attributed the power of Jesus' name over demons, to his paschal mystery. So from earliest times references to the passion became part of the ceremony of exorcism. This was particularly clear in the liturgy of baptism. At a time when it was common for pagan adults to seek this sacrament of initiation, the converts were asked to renounce evil spirits because it was suspected that idol worship might have left them vulnerable to their malign influence. This notion was derived from the Pauline text which said, 'I imply that what pagans sacrifice they offer to demons and not to God.' (1 Cor. 10:20)

Although references to the devil have been rightly reduced in the revised sacramental liturgies, such as the rite of baptism, some remain. Now as in the past, we variously ask for victory over 'Satan,' 'the devil,' and 'the powers of darkness.' The three traditional questions, 'Do you reject Satan? and all his works? and all his empty promises? are still retained. There is also a prayer of exorcism which reads, 'Almighty and ever living God, you sent your Son into the world to cast out the power of Satan, the spirit of evil, to rescue people from the kingdom of darkness and bring them into the splendour of your kingdom of light.' The same is true of the Rite of Christian Initiation of Adults and the Rite for the Catechumenate. All stages of the former include deliverance prayer e.g. pars, 44, 79, 111, and 112. The latter, has introduced many 'minor' exorcisms throughout the period of instruction. Finally, as part of the Easter Vigil, the greatest feast of the liturgical year, the congregation are still invited to renew the baptismal promises mentioned already. As regards the rest of the Church's liturgy, Cipriano Vagaggini, author of the monumental *Theological Dimensions* of the Liturgy, shows how the demonic motif figures not only in the sacraments, but also in about fifty sacramentals as well.

Demonology in Contemporary Theology

The *Irish Report of the European Values Systems Study*, [27] which was published in the eighties, confirms the common sense impression that while 95% of Irish and 75% of European people believe in the existence of God, only 55% of Irish and 25% of European people believe in the existence of a Devil. A more recent update, shows that the number who believe in the devil has fallen a few percentage points over the last ten years.That said, I think that Jules Toner is correct when he says[28] that very few, if any reputable theologians or scripture scholars are willing to *assert* that the existence of angels and evil spirits is certainly not a matter of faith or of revelation. Scholarly opinion seems to adopt two different approaches to the subject.

Differing Theological Views

Firstly, there are those who question whether belief in the Devil is either necessary or relevant in contemporary Christianity. Jesuit theologian Peter Schoonenberg is representative of one school of thought which wonders whether belief in the devil's existence is an article of faith. He points out that 'scripture presupposes rather than affirms the existence of good and evil spirits.' He says much the same about the wording of an important credal statement drawn up at the fourth Lateran Council in 1215. While it states quite clearly that 'The Devil and the other demons were created by God good according to their nature, but they made themselves evil by their own doing,' he goes on to comment, 'even this doctrinal statement, which most explicitly speaks of angels and devils, presupposes but does not directly affirm their existence.'[29]

The legitimacy of this approach has been challenged by Paul Qual in a scholarly examination of the teaching of the fourth Latern Council. He subjects to critical analysis the arguments of those theologians, like Schoonenberg, who hold that the council, like the scriptures, did not intend to define the existence of angels and demons as a matter of faith. He concludes, 'doubts or denials that the existence of angels or devils is an article of Catholic faith have been shown to be without serious grounding. There is no way to restrict the defining intent of IV Latern to merely the universality and unicity of God's creative activity and the creaturely origins of evil.'[30] Henry Kelly ignores these scholarly conclusions and develops Schoonenberg's sceptical argument. He concludes his book on demonology by saying 'Although it is possible that evil spirits exist, at the present time it does not seem probable; but whether or not they exist, it does not appear to be necessary to believe in them in order to cope with the problems of human life. Given the evils that belief in demonology has caused in the past, and given also the uncertainty of its claim to a place in Christian revelation and theology, it would seem best to act as though evil spirits did not exist, until such time as their existence is forced upon us.'[31] I suspect that many of today's Christians would agree with that agnostic and pragmatic conclusion. But is it really justifiable?

As we have already seen, some of the most reputable theologians in the Church, while warning against a crude mythological understanding of the devil and his demons, maintain nevertheless that their existence remains an important but secondary aspect of Catholic teaching and cannot be explained away as merely a personification of evil in the world. For example Karl Rahner has written, 'The existence of angels cannot be disputed in view of the conciliar declarations (D 428, 1783). Consequently it will be firmly maintained that the existence of angels and demons is *affirmed* in Scripture and not merely assumed as a hypothesis which we can drop today.'[32] This view has found an authoritative echo in two relatively recent pronouncements. Speaking at a general audience in 1972, Pope Paul VI said, 'Evil is not merely a lack of something,[33] but an effective agent, a living, spiritual being, perverted and perverting ... It is a departure, from the the picture provided by biblical and Church teaching to refuse to acknowledge the devil's existence...or to explain the devil as a pseudo-reality, a conceptual, fanciful personification of the unknown causes of our misfortunes.'[34]

Sometime later in 1975, a document entitled 'Christian Faith and Demonology' was published. Not only does it note all the objections to demonology mentioned earlier, it denies their validity while reiterating and expanding the Pope's teaching in a more systematic way that takes account of the teaching of scripture and tradition over the centuries. It concludes, 'the position of the Catholic Church on demons is clear and firm. The existence of Satan and the demons has indeed never been the object of an explicit affirmation by the magisterium but this is because the question was never put in those terms. Heretics and faithful alike, on the basis of scripture, were in agreement on the existence and chief misdeeds of Satan and his demons.'[35] It is interesting to note that while Paul VI and the Vatican Document affirm the existence of Satan, they both agree that we know precious little about him. 'Our doctrine becomes uncertain, obscured as it is by the darkness surrounding the devil'[36] observed the Pope, it is 'an enigma surrounding the Christian life'[37] adds the Roman decree.

The Devil in Ascetical Theology

Since New Testament times, spiritual theology has constantly shown how evil powers can impinge in a negative way upon individuals and society. Starting, in particular with Evagrius Ponticus (346-399), the church has developed the art of discernment of spirits, in order to recognise the origin and orientation of thoughts, desires, impulses, inspirations etc. As Cassian said, 'In truth we should be aware above all that our thoughts have three possible sources – God, the devil and ourselves.' These three forms of inspiration are *experienced* within the conscious and/or unconscious psyche. Two of them, however, have their *origin* outside the personality. They are prompted by either the Spirit of God which inclines a person toward deeper relationship with the Lord, or by the evil spirit which sooner or later, inclines a person away from such relationship. By and large, such inspirations are influenced by the life enhancing or life denying elements of the culture in which we live. St Ignatius suggested that the 'enemy of our nature' separates individuals and groups from the Lord by prompting them to desire possessions rather than poverty, reputation rather than humility, autonomy rather than dependence on God.[38] In this way they form that kind of 'false consciousness,' mentioned earlier. Although their lips may still praise the Lord, their hearts will in fact, be far from him (cf Mt 15:8).

Discernment of spirits is necessary to establish whether our inspirations are from God or not. Writers such as Ignatius Loyola, Francis de Sales and J. B. Scaramelli have produced lists of rules for discerning good spirits from bad ones.[39] In general terms, inner movements or inspirations that are prompted by the Holy Spirit will be associated with spiritual consolation i.e. feelings of peace, joy, hope, faith, tears, elevation of soul etc. Movements which are not from God, especially those that are prompted by the evil spirit, will sooner or later, be associated with spiritual desolation i.e. feelings of agitation, loss of peace, sadness, longing for base things, aridity, apathy etc. While writers like Ignatius, believed that evil spirits were personal beings, they don't say much about them. They focused on their effects instead, such as alienation from God, reduction of inner freedom and spiritual disturbance. As far as I am aware, however, there is not a single contemporary book on spiritual direction which denies the existence of evil spirits.

We can note in passing that over the centuries, spiritual theology has offered guidelines to be used when trying to assess strange occurrences where the possibility of spiritual obsession or preternatural phenomena are concerned. For example, some time ago a Jesuit who lectures on the philosophy of religion in a European university, told me how that he had been asked to investigate a case which allegedly involved a poltergeist. He said that having stayed in the house concerned for two days, he had no doubt that scarifying phenomena such as loud noises and furniture moving apparently on its own accord, were occurring there. They didn't stop until every room was exorcised by reading Eph 6:10-17 and offering fervent prayer for deliverance.

More recently, I was consulted about an unusual case involving a four year old child who was regularly disturbed by a man who used to appear to her in her bedroom. It was claimed that these alleged apparitions were associated with things like a drop in room temperature, and the spontaneous combustion of plaster cast statues which failed to leave any burn marks on the wood on which they had been placed. A baby brother who was in the same room was also found to have bruising on his body, although there was no evidence that he had been touched by anyone. When consulted about these happenings, local priests either dismissed the parent's claims on an *a priori* basis, or were at a loss as to what to do. Eventually, the circumstances were so disturbing that the family involved had to leave their flat. If in fact spirits were active, it was obvious that they were associated with the house rather than its occupants because the disturbances ended as soon as they got alternative accommodation.

Jordan Aumann is one of a small minority of reputable theologians who have written insightfully about this kind of issue. For instance he says, 'The authentic manifestations of true diabolical obsession will be sufficiently clear if they are revealed by visible signs such as the moving of an object by an invisible hand, the marks of bruises or wounds that proceed from an invisible attack. These effects cannot be attributed to any purely natural cause, and when the person who suffers them gives all the signs of equanimity, self-possession, sincerity, and true virtue, the director can be certain that he or she is dealing with a case of obsession.'[40] Fortunately, writers like Aumann provide well informed, balanced and helpful assessments of unusual occurrences such as the ones I have briefly described. However, in my experience, very few Christians, including the clergy seem to know much about this rare and obscure corner of ascetical theology. Regrettably, as a result, it is often neglected by the institutional Church and left by default to spiritualists, rationalists, and fundamentalists.

CHAPTER 9

Modern Psychology and the Devil

The rise of science led in the 18th century to the rationalism of the Enlightenment. This trend found symbolic expression when an actress from the Opera, was crowned 'Goddess of Reason' in Notre Dame Cathedral on November 10th. 1793 during the French Revolution. In the 19th. century these trends were championed by two men in particular. Ludwig Feuerbach (d. 1872) in reacting to the philosophical idealism of Hegel, argued that God was nothing but a projection of human potential. As a result he reinterpreted theological beliefs in purely anthropological terms. In his *The Essence of Christianity* he wrote, 'Homo homini Deus est, i.e. man's God is man. This is the highest law of ethics. This is the turning point of world history.'[41] Auguste Comte (d. 1857) maintained in his book *Positive Philosophy*, that history can be divided into three eras, the religious up to about 500 B.C. the philosophical up to around 1500 A.D. and the modern era, the age of scientific positivism. He argued that religious and philosophical forms of knowledge had been rendered redundant by science.

A study of intellectual history since then shows how these two men have had many followers, notably Marx, Nietzche, and Freud. For example the latter's atheism was very much influenced by Feuerbach and Comte. He wrote, 'All I have done – and this is the only thing that is new in my exposition – is to add some psychological foundation to the criticisms of my great predecessors.'[42] Paul Vitz indicates how the attitudes of many 20th century psychologists such as Fromm, May, Rogers and Maslow can be traced back to these influential atheists. So when we study their writings it is worth remembering that by and large they do not believe in a supernatural realm of spirits, or the spiritual validity of phenomena like religious dreams, visions, healings, miracles etc. In other words they deny the legitimacy of Jesus' world view. They tend to reject belief in the supernatural as a form of outdated mythology or as a manifestation of psychological pathology.

For example, when psychiatrists are looking for information they can consult an American publication known as the *Diagnostic and Statistical Manual of Mental Disorders (DSM-3-R)*.[43] Among other things, it describes schizophrenia as 'Odd or bizarre ideation, or magical thinking, e.g. superstitiousness, clairvoyance, telepathy and the 'sixth sense.' Later on it says that the illness involves unusual perceptual experiences, e.g. 'recurrent illusions, *sensing the presence of a force or person not actually present.*' (my italics). Lastly, it states that beliefs or experiences of members of religious or other sub-cultural groups 'may be difficult to distinguish from delusions or hallucinations.' Clearly, the manual might classify many Christian experiences, such as visions, praying in tongues, a sense of diabolical evil, or an awareness of the presence of Christ and the Holy Spirit, as pathological states. Indeed Freud, described religion in general as a 'collective, obsessive neurosis.' With these thoughts in mind I will firstly examine Freudian and Jungian psychology in so far as they relate to demonology, before going on to look at what contemporary psychiatrists have to say about it.

Freud's Critique of Demonology

I think it is true to say that Freud's thinking on the devil matured in the course of his writing. There were two phases. We will look at each. In his earlier work he saw the devil as a projection of the repressed aspects of the unconscious. He argued, as we have already seen, that the personality is structured by the interrelationship if the *id, ego* and *superego.*

- The *id* is the seat of the instincts, an undifferentiated drive which is guided by the pleasure principle e.g. sexual libido. It is a primary process which is largely unconscious and partly revealed in dreams and fantasies.

- The *ego* embraces a person's conscious self-awareness as it relates in a realistic way to outer and inner reality. It includes such things as memory, feeling, judgement, consciously espoused values, beliefs etc. As the executive aspect of personality the ego is a secondary process.

- The *super-ego* represents the internalised values and attitudes of significant others such as parents, teachers and clergy. It manifests itself in the form of a dutiful or moralistic conscience.

121

In Freud's conflict theory of the personality, the *ego* has to mediate between the competing demands of the *id* and the *super-ego*. To satisfy the ethical, and sometimes overweening demands of the super-ego it has to repress the amoral urges of the *id*. Various defense mechanisms are needed to make this possible. Freud argued that it is this repressed instinctual side of our natures which is projected outwards and personified as the devil. He wrote, 'The neuroses of olden times were masquerading in demonical shape and evil spirits were the projection of base and evil wishes into the world.' 44

The Devil and the Oedipal Complex

The thought of the later Freud is more complex and speculative. His attitude to the devil was inextricably linked to his speculations about the origin of the idea of God. Basically, God and the devil are the product of a two way projection of the good and evil elements in a person's father image. Freud, constructed his theory from two related ideas, the notion of a primal father, and the Oedipal conflict with one's actual father. Incidentally in the case of girls he talks about the Electra complex, but by and large his theory is male in its orientation. He explains the concept of projection in his *General Introduction to Psychoanalysis*. The son develops 'a peculiar tenderness' for his mother, the daughter for her father. Both son and daughter respectively, see their father and mother as rivals. Deep down they would like to murder the rival parent in order to marry the desired one. That said, it is also true that children love and admire their parents. So their attitudes are characterised by ambiguity. According to Freud it is the positive and negative aspects of the parental image that are projected outward to form the notions of God and the devil.

Apparently these projections are supposed to resonate with the inherited memory of ancestral sons and their conflict with their tyrannical father who was at once the object of their admiration and their hate. Because he retained the available women for his own sexual needs, and was ruthless with his rivals, the sons decided to murder and devour him. Later the sons suffered from remorse. They tried to avoid a repetition of this original sin in the future. They embraced totemism,45 forbade sexual relations with women in the group, and shared in a totem meal. But after a time the totem meal ceased to serve as a substitute for the primal father. He then became the prototype of God himself. At first this image embraced the good and evil aspects of the father. Later, however, the projection was split, the good aspects being attributed to God, the evil aspects being attributed to the devil. 'Psychoanalysis,' commented Freud, 'has made us familiar with the intimate connection between the father complex and belief in God; it has shown us that a personal God is, psychologically speaking, *nothing other* (my italics) than an exalted father ... thus we recognise that the roots of the need for religion are in the parental complex.' Elsewhere he adds, that such religion is an illusion. And if so, then, 'the devil is certainly nothing else than the personification of the repressed instinctual life.' [46]

An Evaluation of Freud's Views

Now for an evaluation of Freud's theories. The concept of the Oedipus and Electra complexes was of central importance in his critique of religion. However, there are little or no empirical evidence to support his rather strange mythical claims. For example, Hans Kung has pointed out that there is no conclusive evidence which would support the notion of an Oedipus complex. He quotes A. Hoche, a dream researcher who says that neither he nor any other investigator had found proof that men desired their mothers and wanted their fathers killed.

There isn't any evidence, either, to support Freud's fanciful notion of the primeval horde. In this connection Kung quotes some observations of Mircea Eliade, who expressed surprise at the incredible success of Freud's *Totem and Taboo*, in view of the fact that even in his own time the leading scholars, Rivers, Boas, Kroeber, Malinowski and Schmidt, had proved 'the absurdity of such a primordial 'totemic banquet'.' As Kung observes, Freud didn't worry too much about this, his was a theory of religion which he accepted in an a *priori*, unquestioning way and then tried to bolster up with so called evidence. He adds, 'from the indisputable influence of the psychological factor on religion and the idea of God, no conclusions can be drawn about the existence or non-existence of God (or by the same token, the devil) ... psychoanalysis therefore may not reduce all reality to the psychological sphere if it is to avoid the danger of a reductionist hermaneutic.' [47]

It is a curious fact that many Christians have accepted Freud's critique of demonology while retaining their belief in God. He would have been the first to point out the logical inconsistency of such an approach. From a psychological point of view God and the devil are two sides of the same religious coin. If one accepts that the concept of the devil as 'nothing but' a psychological projection of unconscious elements of the personality, by implication so too is the concept of God, and *visa versa*. I do accept however, that if one believes that God exists for philosophical and theological reasons, belief in the devil isn't necessarily implied.

Jung's Understanding of Demonology

Like Freud, Jung's is a conflict theory of the personality, a struggle between the conscious ego and the largely unconscious self and its archetypes e.g. the persona, and the *animus* and *anima*.[48] 'I discriminate,' he wrote in his *Psychological Types*, 'between the ego and the self, since the ego is only the subject of my consciousness, while the self is the subject of my totality; hence it also includes the unconscious psyche. In this sense the self would be a factor which embraces and includes the ego.' [49]

The unconscious self is the home of another psychological archetype, what Jung calls the shadow i.e. the dark, unwanted side of personality which has been repressed to preserve the idealistic and unrealistic self-image of the ego. Jung's notion of the shadow is similar in some respects to Freud's notion of the *id*.[50] When it is neither recognised or accepted, the evil or negative aspects of the psyche are projected on to others. This mechanism would help to explain the irrational dimension of interpersonal relationships, and the related phenomena of prejudice and social conflict.

The Devil and the Shadow Self

Without making metaphysical assertions, Jung sees the projection of the shadow as the source, psychologically speaking, of the concept of the devil. He wrote in his *Psychology of Transference*, 'The Church has the doctrine of the devil, of an evil principle, whom we can imagine complete with cloven hoofs, horns, and tail, half beast, a deity apparently escaped from the rout of Dionysus, the sole surviving champion of the sinful joys of paganism. An excellent picture, and one that exactly describes the grotesque and sinister side of the unconscious; for we have never really come to grips with it and consequently it has remained in its original savage state.'[51] In a footnote Jung is emphatic that he is not dabbling in metaphysics or discussing matters of faith. He commented, 'Whatever religious experience or metaphysical truths may be in themselves, looked at empirically they are essentially psychic phenomena, that is, they manifest themselves as such and must therefore be submitted to psychological criticism, evaluation, and investigation. Science comes to a stop at its own borders.'[52] Jung believed that the rejection of the personal and collective shadow is unfortunate because it robs people of a great inner potential for good. He wrote, 'The unconscious is not just evil by nature, it is also the source of the highest good, not only bestial, semi-human, and demonic, but superhuman, spiritual, and in the classical sense of the term, divine.' [53]

Jung looked at the Christian symbols to see if they were adequate from a psychological point of view, as the objects of religious faith. He seems to have been dissatisfied with two aspects of Catholic thought in particular. Firstly, because a person's shadow is a combination of light and darkness, God as symbol should incorporate these two aspects. The anthropocentric God of the O.T. seemed to do this. As a result, there was little need during that era, for a devil. In the N.T., however, Jesus is the light of the world, there is no darkness in him. Consequently the dark, shadow side of our experience has to be projected on to Satan the Antichrist, who has no relationship with the Trinity. Jung argued that Christianity would need to integrate, good and evil, God and Satan, if it was to provide an adequate symbol for people's innate desire for psyho-spiritual wholeness. Otherwise, a permanent split between good and evil, would continue to reinforce an unhealthy psychic dualism. According to Jung, it is this tragic fracture that explains most of the ills in the world. Having failed to recognise or tame the daimonic aspects of our personal or collective lives, we project them on to individuals and groups whom we demonise. We see and condemn in them what we have failed to see and accept in ourselves. The devil uses this kind of blindness and alienation to instigate the countless evils that afflict our world.

Complexes and the Privatio Boni

Jung's notion of the shadow was augmented by his understanding of unconscious complexes. They are a feature of the personal unconscious, whereby associated groups of feelings, thoughts and memories can cluster together to form a complex which represents a relatively autonomous and powerful sub-personality within the total psyche.[54] Jung's use of the word has passed into common parlance to describe a person who suffers from a 'hang up.' Complexes are natural phenomena which can develop along positive as well as negative lines. Which it will be, depends on the ego's ability to form a viable relationship with the complexes. Otherwise they will lead a life of their own in the unconscious mind from where they can at any moment hinder conscious activity by hijacking people from within. As a result they may end up doing something irresponsible which evokes comments like the following, 'I don't know what came over him,' 'she isn't her real self,' or 'it's just not like him to act like that,' or 'what possessed her to do what she did?' Indeed up to 1919, Jung sometimes wondered whether this notion of the complexes might not be a 'description of primitive demonology.' He felt that when people in ancient and medieval times spoke of possession by a demon, they were referring to either possession by, or repression of complexes.

Secondly, Jung also took issue with Catholic theology's belief that evil is merely *privatio boni* , i.e. the absence of good. Indeed his friendship with Fr White O.P. nearly came to grief over this issue. This influential strand of thinking taken from Aristotle and accepted by Sts Augustine and Thomas, sees evil, not as a substantial entity, but as the absence of a good that should be there. For example, Aquinas wrote, 'To know what badness is you must understand good. Whatever is of value is good, and that includes all natural existence and perfections. Badness then cannot be a particular sort of existence or form of nature; it cannot be anything but the absence of good.'[55] Jung was of the opinion that this notion was linked to the split between good and evil, Christ and Antichrist which we noted already. In one of his letters he wrote, 'On the practical level the *privatio boni* doctrine is morally danger-ous, because it belittles and discounts Evil and thereby weakens the Good, because it deprives it of its necessary opposite. There is no white without black, no right without left, no above without be-low, no warm without cold, no truth without error, no light with-out darkness etc. If Evil is an illusion, Good is necessarily illusory too. That is the reason why I hold that the *privatio boni* is illogical, ir-rational and even nonsense.'[56] Clearly Jung believed that in 'nulli-fying the reality of evil,' Christian theology actually fostered it.

A question arises. Did Jung believe that the devil was a metaphysical as well as a psychological reality? Apparently his thought changed on this subject. Early in his career he was of the opinion that evil spirits were simply unconscious, autonomous complexes that appeared as projections because they were not associated with the ego. In later works he stated bluntly[57] that an exclusively psychological approach could not do justice to the phenomena in question. For example, in a letter to Bill Wilson the founder of Alcoholics Anonymous he wrote, I am strongly con-vinced that ... an ordinary person unprotected by an action from above and isolated in society, cannot resist the power of evil, which is called very aptly the Devil.'[58] At the end of World War II he wrote a psychological study of the Nazi phenomenon, in the course of which he observed, 'Just when people were congratulat-ing themselves on having abolished all spirits, it turned out that instead of haunting the attic or old ruins, the spirits were flitting about in the heads of apparently normal Europeans. Tyrannical, obsessive, intoxicating ideas and delusions were abroad every-where, and people began to believe the most absurd things, just as the possessed do.'[59]

An Evaluation of Jung's Views

How can we evaluate Jung's thinking on demonology? As a scientist he was usually careful in sticking to the scientific method. Normally he avoided the danger of making metaphysi-cal judgements on the basis of psychological facts. However his efforts to reinterpret the Christian doctrines of the Trinity and the devil, fail to observe this rule, and end up in a Gnostic type solution. Very few thinkers accept his belief that because in the self, good and evil are closer than identical twins, Satan and the Trinity should be integrated in some way or other. This is one of the unusual cases where he went, in an unjustifiable fashion, from an empirical description to suggest a metaphysical conclusion. As regards his critique of the doctrine of the *privatio boni*, John Sanford has pointed out that the Catholic interpretation does not deny the reality of evil, rather it defines its nature. While evil exists as an entity, it can only do so by living off the good and cannot exist on its own.[60]

What is significant however, is the fact that like Freud, Jung thought that the notions of God and the devil were inextricably linked from a psychological point of view. Unlike Freud however, he seemed to believe that both God and the devil existed in fact. He avoided the danger of psychological reductionism by acknowledging the existence of a supernatural realm which included good and evil spirits and phenomena like extrasensory knowledge, prophecy, tongues, visions and the healing of people who were demon possessed or physically ill.[61] His analytical psychology shows how these spirits can be subjectively experienced, especially through growing awareness of the personal and collective unconscious. He also believed that people will only succeed in opposing evil when they rely on the grace of God. He wrote, 'Freud has unfortunately overlooked the fact that man has never yet been able single-handed to hold his own against the powers of darkness ... He has always stood in need of spiritual help ... He is never helped in his suffering by what he thinks of for himself: only superhuman, revealed truth lifts him out of distress.' [62]

Demonology and Modern Psychiatry

Modern psychiatry has reflected on the experience of evil. We have already seen the differences that characterise the conflict theories of Freud and Jung. In the sixties Rollo May wrote a book on marriage. In chapters five and six, he examined the daimonic aspect of human experience in a way that is reminiscent of Freud's notion of the id and Jung's concept of the shadow. It resides in everyone, and is good unless it is un-leashed in a non-integrative way. 'The daimonic'[63] he says, is the urge in every being to affirm itself, assert itself, perpetuate and preserve itself ... The daimonic becomes evil when it usurps the total self without regard to the integration of that self, or to the unique forms and desires of others and their need for integration.'[64] He goes on to say that it can reveal itself in excessive aggression, hostility and cruelty, and the things we tend to repress or to project on to others. While May's description of the daimonic aspects of human experience is insightful, he seems to believe that the devil is nothing other than a metaphor for this disturbing aspect of human nature.

I was interested to see however that Dr Elmer Green' of the Menninger Foundation observed that 'Many mental patients have made the claim of being controlled by subjective entities, but the doctors in general regard these statements as part of the behavioural aberration, pure subconscious projections, and do not investigate further.'[65] The Subjective entities, referred to by Dr Green seem to be similar to the notions of May and Jung about 'the daimonic' and 'complexes,' respectively. Dr Green also seems to be suggesting that such complexes or entities may be the points of vulnerability where the evil spirits can occasionally exert their malevolent influence upon the personality. Victor White has shown how the teaching of St Thomas Aquinas can help to explain the subtle interrelationship between the two. 'For Thomas devils can only act upon the human mind through natural, physical and psychological causes; conversly all natural physical causes can be instruments of diabolic purposes.'[66] They probably do this indirectly by exploiting the negative aspects of what sociologists refer to as the 'anonymous powers and systems' of society, such as class divisions, inequalities, injustices and prejudices which have such a distorting but un-recognised influence upon our sense of self, values and beliefs. In other words, evil seems to be the outcome of 'the sin of the world,' a subtle interrelationship of personal and social factors, which can be exploited by the devil.

Subjective Complexes and Social Evil

For example, one could argue that in the North of Ireland, or any country troubled by social conflict, the evil spirits exploit the systemic injustices of society by impinging upon the daimonic or subjective complexes of the unconscious minds of people who feel compelled to perform irrational acts of violence. It is ironic, that many of the same people will try to consciously justify their hateful deeds by talking about abstract ideals, their 'angels of light,' such as national self-determination, freedom, equality, justice etc. Due to a combination of things like presumption and lack of self-awareness they are usually blissfully unaware of their unconscious motives such as envy, resentment, anger, revenge, hatred, prejudice, greed etc. Arthur Koestler once observed that the number of violent crimes committed for consciously base motives fade into insignificance compared to those committed for the greater glory of God so to speak, i.e. out of a self-sacrificing devotion to a flag, a leader, a religious faith or a political conviction.[67]

For example, echoing the views of the late Ernest Becker,[68] an American psychiatrist called Lifton from Yale University, has explained the participation of medical men in the Holocaust in these words, 'Doctors were the embodiment of Nazi political and racial ideology in its ultimate murderous form. The killing came to be projected as a medical operation. 'If you have a gangerous growth, you have to remove it.' If you view the Jews as death-tainted, then killing them seems to serve life. Most killing is not done out of sadism, not even most Nazi killing. *The murders are done around a perverted vision of life enhancement* '[69] (my italics). Nowadays, the legitimacy of abortion is justified with equally fallacious arguments. As Jeanne Manon Roland put it before she was cruelly guillotined during the French Revolution, 'O, Liberty, O Liberty, what crimes are committed in thy name.'

The Relationship Between Sin and Evil

In this sense, evil and sin are not necessarily synonymous. While all sins are evil, not all evils are sinful. I say this because, evil actions or omissions may be performed with little or no knowledge or consent. People can unwittingly do something hateful without really knowing what they are doing e.g. the obvious example of a psychopath who commits a murder. But if we are to believe what some psychologists are saying, there are people who are clinically sane and supposedly responsible for *all* their conscious actions, who may occasionally perform objectively evil deeds on a blind impulse. These so called 'crimes of passion,' are committed with little knowledge and an apparent absence of consent. It's as if their conscious will power had been momentarily set aside by evil forces. From a psychological point of view one could talk about semi autonomous complexes overwhelming people in certain adverse circumstances. From a spiritual point of view one could talk of evil spirits possibly impinging upon such complexes thereby exploiting uncontrolable daimonic potentials in the personality.

For example, a few years ago a Protestant school boy in an Ulster town went to see, *The Exorcist*, a film I have already referred to. A few days later, he apparently saw a black mass being celebrated on a local beach. The next time he attended morning assembly, it became obvious that there was something wrong with him. As soon as the name of Jesus was mentioned during the prayer time, he became hysterical, shouted obscenities, and acted in an aggressive and violent way. One could argue with good reason that his irrational behaviour was 'nothing but,' a psychological problem, one which was rooted perhaps in unresolved childhood conflicts, fears and problems. On the other hand, it could have been one of those rare cases where the evil spirit acts upon already present points of psychic vulnerability to compel weird and uncharacteristic behaviour. In the event, the boy failed to recover until two experienced clergymen prayed with him that he might be delivered from the evil influence which had been oppressing him. Once the spiritual problem had been dealt with successfully, he was free to benefit from any psychotherapy or counselling he might have needed in order to overcome his psychological problems.

This way of looking at evil raises a number of questions. If people's behaviour is clearly evil and sinful from an objective point of view, is it possible that could it be evil, but not sinful from a subjective point of view? Jesus seemed to think so. He excused those who crucified him on account of their ignorance, 'Father, forgive them,' he said, 'they do not know what they are doing' Lk 23:34. Presumably he would have displayed a similar attitude to demonised people who had engaged in immoral activities such as prostitution. (cf Lk 8:2) In their case he could have prayed, 'father forgive them, they have no control over what they are doing.' If this interpretation is correct, couldn't it apply to some contemporary evil and criminal acts. Is it either realistic or just, to hold the perpetrators responsible on the basis that they are sane, fully aware and therefore in control of everything they do? Surely, from a psychological point of view, it may be a case of occasional 'possession' from within by un-acknowledged complexes. From a spiritual point of view, couldn't it be that this type of psychological 'possession,' might be a manifestation, in some instances, of demonic influence or oppression? The answers to these questions determine our attitude to guilt and punishment in court cases, and also to the nature of psycho-spiritual healing and deliverance.

Spiritual Oppression and the Courts

While not wishing to minimise the importance of personal responsibility where sinful wrong-doing is concerned, we need to refine and deepen our understanding of the psychological and spiritual influences that can diminish or negate it altogether. In spite of the fact that modern day courts take account of the notion of diminished responsibility, I suspect that they don't take sufficient account of this point when determining guilt and appropriate punishments.

A man of limited intelligence and education, for example, is the son of a brutal father, and a neurotic mother. In spite of his hurts and deprivations he is a sane and idealistic person with considerable reserves of good-will. But because of unresolved emotional problems of an unconscious kind together with a serious lack of self-awareness and self-esteem, he is very much at risk. His psychic vulnerability can be exposed in circumstances of acute pressure and conflict. For example, after losing his job and suffering a difficult bereavement, he gets into an argument with some male companions. Suddenly he flies into a blind and uncontrollable rage and stabs one of them to death. Sometime later he is found guilty of manslaughter and sentenced to six years in prison. In the name of justice the state authorities may have acted unwittingly, in an unjust way, thereby adding one evil to another.

As Morton Kelsy says, 'Because the law is based upon an antiquated point of view, people who are obviously emotionally incapable of controlling their actions by all modern medical standards are sent to prison and to death by the courts.'[70] Indeed, it has often struck me when visiting men and women in prison, that in spite of their evil actions, some of them were victims from the day they were born, more sinned against than sinners. Instead of helping them to reform, prison only reinforces the psycho-spiritual problems that led to their incarceration in the first place.

Spiritual Oppression and Psychiatry

Because Western psychiatry usually brackets out the importance of the supernatural realm, it puts an exaggerated and misguided emphasis on the complementary tasks of facing reality no matter how painful it is, and of making rational decisions in the light of that encounter. That is O.K. as far as it goes. But if there are spiritual forces oppressing unconscious dimensions of the mind and will, the only way to help such people is to recognise this and to bring a liberating counter-force to bear upon their inner lives. Otherwise they may have a *desire* to do the right thing, but they will not have the power to do so. Only the the Holy Spirit can deliver people from the evil that binds, thereby enabling them to do the good they wish to do. This 'higher power' is normally mediated to oppressed people by means of a relationship with a compassionate and Spirit filled Christian who may, for example, pray with them for deliverance. By 'driving out the evil spirit' in this, and other ways, God's love is free to act therapeutically within the psycho-spiritual dynamics of the liberated self. When it is unimpeded, it has a natural tendency to seek psychic wholeness by means of a growing relationship with God.

It is my belief that this is what Jesus intended when he proclaimed the coming of the Kingdom and healed people, like the deaf and dumb boy, by means of a deliverance prayer. Sadly, the contemporary Church seems to have lost sight of this aspect of the Good News. As a result it tends to overlook the fact that *some* psychiatric patients, for example, will be unable to benifit from medical treatment until they are delivered from spiritual oppression. It seems to me that the Christian community fails in it's responsibility when it refers people with mental illnesses to psychiatric hospitals for treatment, without first identifying whether they are in need of ministry. In any case many psychiatrists are intellectually committed to a reductionist model of human nature, one that takes little or no account of realities such as the soul, God or immaterial spirits. Consequently, it is not surprising that their treatments which are sometimes based on inadequate diagnostic criteria, can fail to achieve satisfactory results. E.C.T. and tranquillisers have no power to deliver a person from oppression by an evil spirit!

Spiritual Oppression and the Church

The church's neglect of the possible need for deliverance ministry is evident even in the sacrament of confession. It can have a marvellously liberating effect as we know. Not only does it forgive sin, it heals people inwardly, thereby providing them with the power to resist temptation and to avoid sin in the future. However, many priests ignore the fact that some of the chronic, soul destroying problems their penitents experience, will only be reversed when they discern the influence of the evil one. If he is oppressing a penitent, in a particular area of his or her life such as a sexual obsession, absolution, counselling and spiritual direction may not be enough. Perhaps the confessor would need to pray for deliverance with expectant faith.[71] Pre-Vatican II textbooks recognised that this kind of ministry was sometimes required and made useful suggestions about how it might be conducted. For example in his *Spiritual Life*, Aldolphe Tanquery wrote, 'If it is morally certain or highly probable that there is diabolical obsession, the spiritual director (or confessor) may make use, in private, the exorcisms contained in the Roman Ritual or of some short formulas. Should he determine to do so, he should not tell the penitent beforehand if he has reason to fear that it would only worry him or her; it will suffice to say that he is going to recite some prayer approved by the Church.' Except for some 'charismatic authors' such as Michael Scanlon,[72] very few contemporary writers advert to the need that sometimes arises in the sacrament of confession, for deliverance prayer.

Differing Attitudes to Possession

Up to now we have been looking at the problem of spiritual oppression i.e. when one aspect of the personality is under the influence of the evil one. It is worth noting that modern psychiatry has conflicting opinions about the notion of possession i.e. when the entire personality seems to be under the influence of the devil. In an article entitled 'Demonical Possession'[73] Peter Gildea has shown how the symptoms which are normally associated with this state, such as convulsions, speaking in unknown tongues, awareness of confidential information about people etc. can be explained in purely psychological terms. Indeed in the 19th. cent. Dr Jean Charcot was able to reproduce the symptoms of possession in hysterical type patients by the use of hypnotism. The Virklers maintain that even without hypnotism a person 'who experiences unusual mental events and begins to believe that he is demon-possessed may act in ways that he understands to be consistent with demon-possession, without conscious simulation on his own part. Such persons may readily manifest all the classical symptoms of demon possession without actually being demon-possessed.'[74] Having assessed the evidence, Peter Gildea concludes, 'There seems to be little, if any doubt, that in every single example, the physical symptoms of possession can have a natural cause and explanation.' Like Rollo May he seems to believe this unusual state is nothing other than 'the traditional name throughout history for psychosis.' Responding to reductionist opinions of this kind, Dr R D. Laing has pointed out that to change 'possession' language for the language of 'complexes' or 'hysterical dissociation' or 'psychosis' may only be a case of exchanging one form of metaphorical wording with another. All language is symbolic, and the symbol is not the reality.

In his book, People of the Lie, Dr Scott Peck states an alternative point of view. While he would readily accept that many possession cases can be explained and treated in exclusively psychological ways, there are others which involve more than a psychological pathology. He says that as a psychiatrist he came to this conclusion as a result of observing a couple of exorcisms. He comments, 'As a hardheaded scientist – which I assume myself to be – I can explain 95 percent of what went on in these two cases by traditional psychiatric dynamics.'[75] He says that the other 5 percent could only be accounted for by believing that it was due to the influence of an evil spirits. These conclusions confirmed what he had already read in Malachi Martin's book, Hostage to the Devil, which contained five detailed case histories of exorcisms. In this

chapter, I'm not so interested in describing the whys and where-
fores of possession, as in establishing that reputable psychiatrists
who are well aware of the dynamics of mental illness believe that
the devil and evil spirits exist, and can impinge upon the human
personality.

CHAPTER 10

Resisting Evil Firm in Faith

We have seen how modern secularist culture tends to reject any reality that cannot be grasped by the senses and understood by reason. However, Michael Ramsay a former Archbishop of Canterbury, rightly observed that 'It is arbitrary to assume that we human beings are the only rational beings, knowing good and evil, in the universe, and it seems to me a reasonable assumption that there are, outside the human sphere, beings who can do good and do evil.'[76] Surely our brief survey of the evidence indicates that Paul VI was correct when he said, 'It is a departure from the picture provided by biblical and Church teaching to refuse to acknowledge the devil's existence ... or to explain the devil as a pseudo-reality, a conceptual, fanciful personification of the unknown causes of our misfortunes.'[77] While the Pope wasn't speaking *ex cathedra* – he rarely does – surely his words have to be respected by Catholics as informed and highly authoritative.

The Devil as a Mythical Creature

We noted that one of the greatest theological objections to belief in the validity of the devil's existence is the fact that scripture and most of tradition speak about him in mythological language. The words 'myth' and 'mythological' can be understood in two different ways. In the *Oxford English Dictionary*, we are told that a myth is a fictitious narrative usually involving supernatural persons, actions, or events and embodying some popular idea concerning natural historical phenomena. Understood in this way the devil could be seen as unreal and insubstantial as a leprechaun or unicorn; merely an imaginative metaphor for the experience of evil. In our time, an influential scripture scholar R Bultmann has adopted this approach. He says that 'The whole conception of the world which is presupposed in the preaching of Jesus and the New Testament is generally mythological.'[78] He goes on to say that its conception of such things as heaven and hell, miracles, demons and the intervention of supernatural powers in the course of events etc. should be rejected as false in our scientific age. Bultmann suggests that the modern Church should preach a gospel message that is stripped of its mythological elements in contemporary language e.g. that of existentialist philosophy.

Alternatively, myths can be understood as symbolic stories which disclose something of the inner meaning of life and reality. As A. K. Coomaraswamy has written, 'Myth embodies the nearest approach to absolute truth that can be stated in words.'[79] Looked at from this point of view demonology can be demythologised in such a way that the devil and his demons may be understood in purely conceptual terms. Theologically they could be viewed as 'Beings who try to hinder our salvation,' psychopathologically as 'unconscious complexes,' and sociologically as 'anonymous powers and systems' as we noted earlier. However, conceptualisations like these are inadequate because demonic evil is essentially irrational a 'mystery of iniquity,' to use a Pauline phrase. While it may be identifiable, it is at the same time essentially incomprehensible, from a purely intellectual point of view.

Encountering the Devil

To combat the devil effectively, we need to move beyond superficial labelling, in order to come to terms with that inner and outer realm of darkness which is the haunt of evil spirits. This can be done in a subjective way, through the mediating power of myths as symbolic expressions of the shadow side of the personal and collective unconscious. 'With a little self-criticism,' Jung wrote, 'one can see through the shadow, in so far as its nature is personal. It is quite within the bounds of possibility for a person to recognise the relative evil of his or her nature, but is a rare and shattering experience for such a person to gaze into the face of absolute evil.' Presumably, this is what Jesus did, when he was tempted by Satan in the wilderness. While the traditional notion of the devil can be stripped of its superstitious and more outlandish accretions, it still needs to be retained in a mythological form so that its content might be encountered in a symbolic way e.g. by means of dreams. Many saintly people such as Padre Pio seem to have had particularly disturbing confrontations with the realm of evil. On January 18th., 1913 he wrote to a colleague about one of his weird diabolical experiences. The demons appeared to him 'in the most abominable form.' When he refused to do their bidding, he said, 'they hurled themselves upon me, threw me on the floor, struck me violently, and threw pillows, books, and chairs through the air and cursed me with exceedingly filthy words.'[80] Perhaps Padre Pio's renowned ability to help people in the confessional was a fruit of this on-going struggle with the powers of darkness. St Antony of the Desert has insisted that the only way for anyone to grow in the gift of discernment, is to have direct experience of the promtings of good and evil spirits.

If evil is neither acknowledged or resisted in this way, it will tend to take people, groups and even nations by surprise. The evil spirit will try to exploit the social inadequacies and the shadow side of the personal and collective unconscious with all its complexes and daimonic energies in order to produce uncontrolled splurges of selfish, irrational and destructive behaviour e.g. incest, abortion, rape, torture, murder, war etc. This will be most inclined to happen during times of personal or social instability and regression. Robert Waite's biography of Hitler, entitled, *The Psychopathic God* [81] is a chilling study of how a person who grew up in a troubled society and was hurt and abused as a child, could become one of the arch destroyers of the twentieth century.

The Danger of a Fundamentalist Approach

If denial of the devil's existence is one extreme to be avoided, an inflated estimation of his power and influence is another. Many fundamentalist Christians tend to have a dualistic world view. Either a person's inspirations come from the Spirit of God or the evil spirit. As a result they tend to underestimate the importance of human responsibility and the fact that many if not most of our inspirations originate in the conscious or unconscious mind. It is not surprising therefore that having wrongly attributed to the evil spirit, things like ungodly attitudes and actions, they go on to perform a simple or solemn exorcism, when confession of sin, compassionate counselling, or psychotherapy would have been more appropriate. Not only can this simplistic and ill-informed approach to the devil's influence have detrimental effects on the person who is being ministered to, it can also bring the Church's nuanced belief in demonology into disrepute. Ironically, such an outcome can itself be exploited by the 'adversary' with bad effects. Catholic theology stresses quite rightly, that many if not most of our inspirations come from our own natures with all their limitations and sinful tendencies. As Cardinal Leon-Joseph Suenens has pointed out, the deliverance we need is not so much from the devil, as from the sin at work with us, which makes us it's slaves and diminishes our freedom.[82] It not only weakens our relationship with God, it also strengthens Satan's hold on this world because of its nihilistic and antisocial nature.

Clearly in our all important battle with sin, we need to 'test the spirits,' 1 Jn 4:1 that inspire our thoughts, words and deeds. As we develop the art of discernment, we will be able to detect false inspirations as we discriminate between those negative impulses that originate in our wounded and sinful natures, and those which seem to have been prompted by the evil one. It is important to stress that such discernment is motivated by a desire to be 'guided by the Spirit,' Gal 5:25, rather than an exaggerated or morbid preoccupation with the devil and his power. On the contrary the focus of our attention is emphatically on the victorious Christ. It is in the light of our faith in his Lordship over our lives, that we perceive the role of the devil and the unclean spirits. Sometimes, we may have a suspicion, as we have mentioned already, that some of the problems we encounter either in our own lives or the lives of people we meet e.g. self-destructive tendencies, and obsessional behaviours, cannot be understood merely in terms of sinfulness, and psychopathology. In cases like these it may be that the person is being oppressed by an evil spirit. As I have already suggested, no amount of therapy will alleviate the problem, until its spiritual dimension is recognised and dealt with, either by means of deliverance prayer or solemn exorcism. Thankfully, the latter is rarely if ever needed. In any case no matter what the situation is, we realise that although the devil 'prowls around like roaring lion seeking someone to devour,' 1 Pt 5:8 he is a fallen creature, angelic in nature it is true, but no match for God. So we 'resist him firm in our faith,' 1 Pt 5:9 in the sure knowledge that he will flee from us, for 'he who is in us (the Holy Spirit) is greater than he who is in the world, (the evil spirit)' 1 Jn 4:4.

An Illustrative Case Study

A number of years ago I visited Albany in upper state New York. During my short time there, a nursing sister from one of the local hospitals, came to see me. Apparently, both she and her fellow nurses were of the opinion that one of their patients, an elderly woman, was a thoroughly evil person. 'She is so bad,' commented the sister, 'that some of the women who had given up going to Mass, have returned to the sacraments because they are so afraid of her.' 'Surely, as a baptised person,' I responded, 'she herself couldn't be evil, no matter how bad her attitude and behaviour might be.' 'You don't know her father,' she replied, 'we are all agreed that there is something evil about her. Even when we give her tranquillising drugs, they don't seem to have any effect. We have never come across anyone like her.' I went on to enquire, 'If you think she is such a bad person, have any of you prayed for her, so that she might recover a sense of inner peace?' The sister paused a moment, and then replied in an embarassed tone of voice, 'Now that you mention it father, no we havn't. The thought never even entered our minds.' 'Well, why don't you do so in the future. Perhaps this unfortunate woman is being oppressed and disturbed by an evil spirit. If you pray with faith in the name of Jesus, commanding whatever it is to leave her, you can be sure that the Lord will deliver her and restore her to peace.' Having discussed this possibility for a while, the nurse said she would be afraid to do such a thing and we parted company.

A short time later she came to see me again. 'I have been thinking about what you said, father,' she explained, 'I'm willing to pray as you suggested, but before doing so, will you pray for me, and ask the Lord to strengthen me inwardly with his Spirit?' Having done so, I made some further suggestions about the way in which she might minister to the woman in the hospital, and said, 'Please write to me in Boston, and let me know how you got on.' I never saw that sister again, but a month later I received a letter from her. It explained, that when she went to see the woman she was as bad as ever. Sister reached out her hand and placed it on the patient's forehead and silently prayed a prayer of deliverance, followed by a heartfelt request that God would fill her with his Spirit and give her his peace. 'It was like magic,' she wrote, 'I no sooner said the prayer, when the woman immediately became quite and serene. Then three hours later there was an emergency. Doctors and nurses rushed to the bedside of the very woman I had prayed with some time before. In spite of their efforts to revive her, she slipped away. In his providence, God had enabled her to die in peace. I want to thank you for encouraging me to pray for her. Not only did it help her, it showed me as never before that if we trust in the Lord we can literally drive out evil spirits in his name.' I must say that whole episode made a deep impression on me, it was like a parable for our troubled times. It seemed to say that in our secular, scientific culture, we should not ignore the realm of the supernatural and those spirits, good and bad, that can mysteriously impinge upon our lives. It also convinced me, that we Christians need to discern when and if a troubled person might need a prayer to be delivered from the mystery of evil.

Mending the breaches

We live in disturbing times. The walls of both our personal lives and the Church have been breached by an all pervasive, but often unrecognised worldliness which is alien to gospel values. As a result the enemy of our nature surreptitiously enters our lives under the cloak of darkness. Like a latter day Trojan horse he exploits breaches, the points of greatest weakness and vulnerability, in order to mount an insidious attack on the people of God. The serpent's tail is everywhere to be seen in the injustices, perversions and violence of society. Often in the name of liberal democracy and pluralism, he exploits the moral relativism of our age. As Cardinal Suenens has noted 'In matters such as precocious sexual relations, information about contraception for all purposes, procured abortion, sexual deviations, lesbianism and homosexuality, juvenile cohabitation, trial marriage, the very idea that all these forms of behaviour are not left to the whims of men, that there is a divine law, a Word of God, interpreted by the Magisterium, seems to have become quite alien to the conscience of many Christians, who are more concerned with modernisation than with fidelity to doctrine.'[83] If like the prophet Nehemiah, we wish to rebuild the breached walls of our own lives and those of the Church a number of things will be needed.

Ten Ways of Resisting the Evil One

Firstly, we need to ask ourselves this question posed by Walter Burghart, 'For all you know about God, do you really know God? Can you say that, like Ignatius Loyola, you have truly encountered God, the living and true God? Can you say that you know God himself, not simply human words that describe him?'[84] To have a deep personal relationship with Jesus as the Lord of one's life, is to have a shield which will protect one from all the wiles of the evil one. The apostle Peter says, 'Resist him (the devil) standing firm in the faith.' James echoes these words when he says, 'Submit yourselves to God. Resist the devil, and he will flee from you' Jm 4:7. As we rely on God's protecting power we are assured in these words, 'Do not be afraid! Stand by and see the salvation of the Lord which he will accomplish for you today ... The Lord will fight for you while you keep silent' Ex 14:13.

Secondly, because the devil is a liar in whom there is no truth, we need to know the truth about ourselves and Him who is the Truth. The path-way to self-awareness is an arduous one. I have suggested elsewhere[85] how a person might embark on that journey. If we become aware of hurting memories and dysfunctional emotions we need to pray for inner healing and the power to forgive those who may have injured us in the past. Otherwise we will remain vulnerable to the secret influence of the evil one. We also have to fill our minds and hearts with the truth of God's word and the official teaching of the Church. We can do this by means of reading, reflection and frequent prayer, firm in the belief that the Spirit of truth will lead us into the truth about God as Jesus promised in Jn 16:13. It is this truth that sets us free from the deceptions and falsehoods of the evil one

Thirdly, every sin strengthens Satan's hold on this world. St John reminds us that, 'Whoever lives sinfully belongs to the devil, since the devil has been a sinner from the beginning,' 1 Jn 3:8. So in the words of scripture 'You must give up your old way of life, you must put aside your old self, which gets corrupted by following illusory desires. Your mind must be renewed by a spiritual revolution so that you can put on the new self that has been created in God's way,' Eph 4:22-23. One method of doing this is to follow steps four and five of Alcoholics Anonymous, namely, by making a fearless inventory of the unconfessed sins in one's life and by admitting them to oneself, to God and to another human being, e.g. a priest in the sacrament of reconciliation. It is important to resolve with the help of God's grace not to sin in the future and to avoid the occasions of sin, whatever they might be. In this way one engages in a process of on-going and often painful repentance.[86] As Jim Wallis has written, 'Repentance is seeing our sin and turning from it; faith is seeing Jesus and turning toward him. Together repentance and faith form the two movements of conversion.'[87]

Fourthly, conversion involves a willingness to renounce involvement in the occult i.e. knowledge of a secret and mysterious kind which is gained by availing of such things as witchcraft, magic, palmistry, astrology, tarot cards, ouija boards etc. As far as I'm aware the so called New Age Movement has quite an occultish dimension. The scriptures, however, are adamantly opposed to all such forms of esoteric knowledge. They see them as the antitheses of true religion in so far as they seek to know and control human destiny without regard to God's providence, or his Lordship over history past, present and to come. Apart from the psychological problems that can result from participation in occult practices, they can also open a person at an unconscious level, to the disturbing influence of the evil one. So not surprisingly we read in Lev 19:26, 'You shall not practice divination or witchcraft,' and in Deut 18:10, 'No one shall be found among you who makes a son or daughter pass through fire, or who practices divination, or is a soothsayer, or an augur, or a sorcerer, or one who casts spells, or who consults ghosts or spirits, or who seeks oracles from the dead. For whoever does these things is abhorrent to the Lord.' This biblical teaching is repeated in the first century document, *The Didache* when it says, 'Have nothing to do with witchcraft, astrology, or magic; do not even consent to be a witness of such practices, for they too can breed idolatory.'[88] So like the people at Ephesus we need to renounce anything connected with the the occult. Luke tells us what happened, 'A number of those who practiced magic collected their books and burned them publicly' Acts 19:18-20.

Fifthly, we need a growing awareness of how the evil spirit tempts people, in the firm belief that if we rely completely on God, he will not allow us to be tempted beyond our strength.

As St Paul has said, 'God is faithful, he will not let you be tempted beyond what you can bear. But when you are tempted he will provide a way out so that you can stand up under it' 1 Cor 10:13. St Ignatius has suggested that the evil one tries to separate us from the Lord by promting firstly a worldly desire for riches, then for reputation, and finally *de facto* if not conscious autonomy from God. He says that the tempter will act either like a bully who intimidates, a seducer who likes secrecy, or a military commander who exploits our principal weakness. We can resist his suggestions by courageously opposing his promptings with God's help, humbly revealing our struggles to a director, confessor or confidant and being prudently on guard in those areas of personal weakness where we know ourselves to be most at risk. [89]

Sixthly, besides having a knowledge of the devil's overall strategy we also need an experiential ability to discern his presence and tactics. Otherwise, we are likely to be at his mercy. A number of things can help in this regard. For example, I begin each day with a prayer to the Holy Spirit which contains the following words, 'Preserve me this day from all illusions and false inspirations.' Like many others, I have also found that it is good to augment this prayer by carrying out a regular examen of consciousness. For example, you could use the following three reflection points. 'Father in heaven, help me to recall with gratitude those occasions when I was aware of your presence today and to savour again what you meant to me ... Help me to become aware of the promptings and inspirations you have given me today and to know whether I responded to them or not ... Enlighten my heart to recognise any selfish and un-loving mood, attitude, desire, impulse or action that saddened your Holy Spirit today.' To have a skilled spiritual director even for a while, or to do a directed retreat, can also help one to grow in the art of discernment of spirits.

Seventhly, like Moses (Ps 106:23) we need to stand in the breach, the place of insecurity and to intercede on a regular basis for divine protection for ourselves and for the Church.[90] As Pope John Paul said at Limerick in 1979, 'Dear sons and daughters of Ireland, pray, pray not to be led into temptation. I asked in my first encyclical for a great, intense and growing prayer for all the Church ... Pray as Jesus taught us to pray: 'Lead us not into temptation but deliver us from evil.' We do so in the firm belief that

145

'the gates of hell shall not prevail against it' Mt 16:18. In this regard many people still like to say the following prayer to St Michael. 'Holy Michael, Archangel, defend us in the day of battle; be our safeguard against the wickedness and snares of the devil. May God rebuke him, we humbly pray: and do thou, prince of the heavenly host, by the power of God thrust down to hell Satan, and all wicked spirits who wander through the world for the ruin of souls. Amen. Besides offering a general prayer like this, one needs to focus on specific areas where the Church and its members are vulnerable to the influence of evil, while interceding that the Lord will be their protection.

Eightly, when St Francis of Assisi, heard a voice say, 'Repair my falling house,' he set about the symbolic task of rebuilding the half ruined church of San Damiano. Like him, we need to respond to God's urgent call to engage in the difficult, but essential job of rebuilding the breached walls of our own spiritual lives and those of the Church. As Nehemiah said, 'You see what a sorry state we are in: Jerusalem is in ruins and its gates have been burnt down. Come on, we must rebuild the walls of Jerusalem and put an end to our humiliating position!' And I told them how the kindly hand of God had been over me ... At this they said, 'Let us start building at once! ... The God of heaven will grant us success ... and they set their hands to the good work' Neh 2:17-20. We need to identify how the Trojan horse of secularism has surreptitiously entered our own personal lives and the life of the Church. We also need to recognise, renounce and reform those ways of thinking and acting which owe more to the ways of the world than they do to the teaching of Christ and his Church.

Ninthly, we need to identify and change the 'autonomous powers and systems' already mentioned, i.e. those aspects of our culture and society which are seed beds of evil. This is a huge subject. Suffice it to say that we need a prophetic protest against the irrational, unchristian attitudes, values and beliefs that inform our secular culture such as exaggerated nationalism, ethnic prejudices, inordinate greed, sexual permissiveness, the 'ressentiment' mentioned earlier etc. We also need to identify social injustices such as unacceptable levels of unemployment, that maintain and even widen the gap between the have's and have not's. It is pretty obvious, that things like poverty, poor housing and lack of dignity, opportunity and hope etc. can have a disruptive effect upon family life with all kinds of knock on effects of a moral kind. As we well know, the devil can exploit evils like these with disastrous results.

Finally, we should praise the Lord at all times in the firm belief that he is greater than anything we might fear, including the devil. As St Paul triumphantly proclaimed, 'Who will separate us from the love of Christ? Will hardship, or distress, or persecution, or peril, or sword? ... No, in all these things we are more than conquerors through him who loved us. For I am convinced that neither angels, nor rulers, nor things present, nor things to come, nor powers, nor height, nor depth, nor anything else in creation, will be able to separate us from the love of God in Christ Jesus our Lord' Rm 8:35-39.

Conclusion

This chapter has looked at scriptural, liturgical and theological reasons for asserting that belief in the devil's existence is an article of the Catholic faith. It has also indicated that while some people use the notion of psychological projection to explain away the existence of Satan, some eminent psychologists and psychiatrists have not only helped to confirm the Church's belief, they have also helped us to understand some of the ways in which the evil one might impinge upon the human personality. Besides indicating how the devil can prompt false inspirations and tempt people to sin, we have also examined the possible dynamics of what is called spiritual oppression and possession. We have noted, in a tentative and provisional way, how they may often involve a subtle interplay between social evils and personal factors, such as unconscious complexes, which, despite their negative and life-denying effects, usually go unrecognised. Even when the 'tail of the serpent' does become apparent, there is nevertheless, something enigmatic and elusive about his existence and activity.[91] As a result, I believe that there will always be something unsatisfactory and frustrating about any study of demonology. That said, it is my belief that depth psychology has still a good deal of insight to contribute to this difficult but important subject.

147

PART 4

Faith and Eucharistic Healing

Almighty and everlasting God, look down in mercy upon me, your servant, who now and again draws near to the most holy sacrament of our only-begotten Son, our Lord Jesus Christ. I approach as one who is sick, to the Physician of life; as one unclean, to the Fountain of mercy; as one blind, to the Light of eternal brightness; as one poor and needy, to the Lord of heaven and earth.'

(*Roman Missal*, Prayer of St Thomas Aquinas before Mass, thirteenth century.)

CHAPTER 11

The Healing Bandage of God

A few years ago I conducted a mission on the outskirts of Cork City. Sometime after the closing Mass, I joined the clergy for Sunday lunch. We were discussing how the week had gone when the parish priest said, 'I met Jimmy McCarthy a while ago when I was walking up and down, reading my office outside the church. Apparently, he was on his way back from the newsagents where he had just bought a packet of cigarettes. As he nervously opened the cellophane, he said to me, 'Father, I need a smoke after what happened during Mass this morning.' When I asked him to explain, he replied, 'Father, you know that I'm not a very religious person, that's why I don't know what to think. When the host was raised at the consecration just a while ago, I looked up and all I could see was a heart beating in the hands of the priest. I was sure it was an optical illusion, so I closed my eyes, shook my head, and took a second look, but it was still there. The same was true when the chalice was raised. All I could see was a heart, beating in the hands of the priest.' 'I know Jimmy quite well,' said the P.P. with a knowing smile, 'Its quite true that he isn't gospel greedy, but I have little doubt that he has had a genuine religious experience. He doesn't know what to make of it, or how to integrate it into the rest of his life. But I suspect that in time, it will have quite an effect upon him.' We all laughed good humouredly, continued eating and quickly changed the topic of conversation.

For my part I was deeply impressed by what we had heard and thought about it afterwards. While I didn't know how to explain what had happened to Jimmy from a psychological point of view, it struck me that he had probably been favoured with a quasi-mystical insight into the fact that the eucharist is *the* sign, source and focus of God's love in the Church and in our lives. As the fourth eucharistic prayer says of Christ, 'He always loved those who were his own in the world. When the time came for him to be glorified by you his heavenly Father, he showed the

150

depth of his love.' It is this wonderful sacramental love that emanates like a stream from the pierced side of the crucified One, so
that it might flow into the world 'for the healing of the nations'
Rev 22:2. Only the waters of God's unrestricted and unconditional
love can satisfy the deepest thirst of the human heart bringing as
it does, salvation, and healing of spirit, mind and body. Appropriately, one document has stated, 'The most blessed eucharist contains the Church's entire spiritual wealth, that is, Christ himself ...
Through his very flesh, made vital and vitalising by the Holy Spirit,
he offers life to people.'[1] It is this life, that like previous generations, we need so much.

The Eucharist Source of New Life

In spite of its frequent triumphs, modern medicine is unable to cure many ailments of mind and body. As suffering people
discover this, it is not surprising that they not only turn to alternative forms of treatment such as acupuncture, homoeopathy, reflexology and osteopathy, they sometimes resort to some of the
more bizarre forms of New Age therapy, in the hope that they will
bring them relief and healing. Many of the same people are devout Christians who attend church on a regular basis. While they
expect to receive spiritual help from the sacraments, normally
they are not encouraged to expect healing of mind or body. For
example, I have noticed during services for the anointing of the
sick, that while many homilists rightly stress the comforting power
of the sacrament, they fail to emphasise its healing potential. As a
result, not unexpectedly many suffering people look for non sacramental forms of relief. They travel to Marian shrines such as
Lourdes and Knock, seek out relics, go to healers, pray to Padre
Pio and so on. While there may be nothing necessarily wrong
with these approaches to healing, it has often struck me that it is a
pity that the official Church has sometimes failed to recognise or
to promote the therapeutic power of it's sacraments. During an
eight year period conducting parish missions around Ireland, I
came to appreciate the healing potential of many of the sacraments e.g. confession, marriage and the anointing of the sick. In
this chapter, however, I would like to focus on the eucharist in
particular, in order to highlight it's ability to bring healing not
only to the human spirit, but to mind and body as well.

A few years ago I was conducting a retreat for some lay people in London. On the last day we had a sharing session. Toward the end, Lucy, a middle aged woman told us her remarkable story. Apparently, she entered a convent when she was eighteen. Then the night before her final profession she upped and left without any bye or leave from anyone. Although she felt terribly guilty about her impulsive departure she never returned. Sometime later she fell in love and married. Tragically her first child died shortly after birth. Lucy believed – quite mistakenly of course – that God was punishing her for abandoning her religious vocation. She continued to believe this, in spite of the fact that her second child survived and grew up enjoying good health. As the years passed her unresolved sense of guilt led to all kinds of neurotic problems. She developed severe agoraphobia. Because she was afraid of going outdoors she became a prisoner in her home, unable to visit friends, attend church, or to do her shopping. This went on, as far as I can remember, for about fifteen years.

Eventually Lucy was feeling so anxious and depressed that she decided to take her own life. She saved up loads of pills with the intention of taking an overdose. Then one day in a fit of despair and desperation she got up, left her house and walked down the street in a daze. As she passed her parish church some instinct drew her inside. Mass was in progress. Lucy knelt at the back with a silent scream of pain welling up within her. By now the priest had reached the consecration. As he extended his hands above the gifts and called on the Holy Spirit to fall upon them, Lucy felt as if a bolt of lightening had hit her. A surge of energy passed through her body. She experienced an inward sense of heat and tingling. This went on for a few minutes. By the time it began to die down, Lucy was a changed woman. Instead of feeling morbid, oppressive guilt, she felt loved and cherished by an incredibly merciful God. Not only that, her depression had lifted, her agoraphobia had disappeared, and she felt an inward sense of peace and joy. It was if she were born again. In fact she was so changed by this Damascus Road experience that her husband found her very hard to cope with. Instead of being a dependent invalid as heretofore, she was now self-possessed and confident.

I must confess, that as I listened to this story I found it

quite awe-inspiring. I was particularly impressed when Lucy described, how, just as she was crying out from the depths of her brokenness, the priest at that very moment was invoking the power of God to come upon the gifts. As the Holy Spirit fell upon the bread and wine thereby transforming them into the body and blood of Christ, the same Holy Spirit fell upon Lucy in a way that transformed her as a person, by healing her in mind and spirit. Rightly, has Jean Vannier remarked, 'The Holy Spirit, the Paraclete, is God's answer to the cry of the broken human heart.' After hearing Lucy's remarkable testimony, I often reflected on it's theological and pastoral implications, in the belief that it would enable me to deepen my understanding of the nature of eucharistic healing.

Jesus our Scapegoat and Liberator

The first thing that occurred to me was the fact that the extension of the priest's hands over the gifts during Mass was reminiscent of the Old Testament notion of scapegoating. This curious ritual was associated with the the Day of Atonement when one of two goats that had been chosen by lot was sent alive into the wilderness, the sins of the people having being laid symbolically upon it. The other was appointed to be sacrificed. We are told that a priest should bring 'a live goat and laying both hands upon its head, confess over it all the sins of the people of Israel. He shall lay all their sins upon the head of the goat and send it into the desert ... and so a goat shall carry all the sin of the people into a land where no one lives' Lev. 16:21-23.

Later in the Old Testament Isaiah points in a prophetic way, to Jesus, as the definitive scapegoat. The sins of the people will be laid upon him, he will carry them on their behalf, so that they might be forgiven. 'The Lord has laid on him the iniquity of us all ... the righteous one my servant, shall make many righteous' Is. 53:5;11. St Paul was to echo this sentiment when he wrote, 'For our sake God made him to be sin who knew no sin, so that in him we might become the righteousness of God' 2 Cor 5:21. However Isaiah goes beyond the teaching of the book of Leviticus which had merely stressed the scapegoat's ability to carry away the sins of the people. The Suffering Servant on the other hand would also bear the sufferings and diseases of the people so that they might experience healing of mind and body. 'Surely he has bourne our infirmities and carried our diseases,' writes the prophet, 'and we have been healed by his bruises' Is 53:4;5. Later St Peter was to endorse these words when he wrote, 'Through his bruises you have been healed' 1 Pt 2:25.

When finally he came, Jesus was motivated by compassion to *proclaim* the good news of God's merciful love. Not only were the ordinary people of his day oppressed from a human point of view, they also felt cut off from God. They were unable to carry the heavy yoke of the law which had been laid upon their shoulders by the authorities in Jerusalem. Jesus was anointed in the Spirit to show God's love to the poor who felt that they had fallen hopelessly short of what the Lord expected of them. He said that God's salvation and liberation were at hand. The Lord was breaking into their lives and was pouring out his unconditional and unrestricted love. The debt of sin was being cancelled. All the people had to do was to look into the eyes of God's mercy, expecting only mercy and they would receive only mercy.

As one of the Hasidim,[2] – an identifiable group of charismatic holy men who bore witness to the loving mercy of God – Jesus was motivated by compassion to *demonstrate* the truth of his proclamation, by performing deeds of power. Perhaps he was aware of a saying of Hanina Ben Dosa, one of his contemporaries who maintained that, 'He whose actions exceed his wisdom, his wisdom shall endure, he whose wisdom exceeds his deeds, his wisdom shall not endure.'[3] Not content with proclaiming the good news of the kingdom in his preaching, Jesus witnessed to it in two main ways, firstly, in his loving deeds e.g. talking at length to the people who followed him into the wilderness, (cf Mk 6:34) and secondly, by performing exorcisms, healings and miracles. As St Peter was to say of him, 'You know about Jesus of Nazareth and how God poured out on him the Holy Spirit and power. He went everywhere doing good and healing all who were under the power of the devil, for God was with him' Acts 10:38. In an influential book, Morton Kelsey has written, 'If Jesus had any one mission it was to bring the power and healing of God's creative, loving Spirit, to bear upon the moral, mental and physical illnesses of the people around him.'[4]

Jesus, the Bandage of God

Jesus' desire to proclaim and demonstrate the good news of God's redeeming love came to a poignant climax during passion week, especially during the Last Supper and the crucifixion. Paradoxically, it was when he was no longer able to preach or exercise his charismatic powers that he bore the most eloquent witness to the unrestricted and unconditional love of God. By accepting his sufferings, crucifixion and death in a spirit of faith and obedience Jesus became God's scapegoat *par excellence* taking upon himself the sins and sufferings of mankind, so that he might become the source of forgiveness and healing for all who would believe in him. As Paul exclaimed, 'The message about the cross is foolishness to those who are perishing, but to those who are being saved it is the power of God' 1 Cor 1:18. It is this same sacrifice of redeeming love that is sacramentally actualised each time the eucharist is celebrated.

Some time ago when I was meditating on this mystery of salvation, I happened to recall an occasion in my childhood when I got a nasty wound in my leg. I had been climbing a tree. A branch broke and a piece of wood stuck into a thigh muscle. My mother removed it as soon as I got home and dressed the wound. Sometime later when it started going septic, my late father, a vet, made a poultice which was designed to draw out the infection while disinfecting and healing the damaged tissues. In the event it was very effective. Then it occurred to me, that Christ our scapegoat, is God's poultice. He not only enfolded our woundedness on the cross, he continues to do so. It is moving to think that Christ the innocent one, was in a sense willing to absorb the evil, of our sin and suffering into himself. On Calvary this unparalleled act of compassion was symbolised by the darkness that enveloped him as his life blood ebbed away, 'It was now about noon, and darkness came over the whole land until three in the afternoon' Lk 23:44. It was as if Christ assimilated all that alienated us from God and wholeness into himself, as he sank firstly into the dark night of the soul and then into Sheol, the dwelling place of the living dead. As he did so he gave us the wonderful light of his forgiveness and healing.

The Eucharist and Forgiveness

The atoning role of Christ the scapegoat is made present in a sacramental way every time we celebrate the Eucharist. The prayers we use, make it abundantly clear that this the greatest of God's gifts to the church, is a Spirit filled proclamation and demonstration of the saving mercy which Christ manifested both in his ministry and in his death on the cross. Like a divine bandage the eucharist is wrapped around the lives of wounded believers in order to bring each and every one of them the forgiveness of the Lord. This is highlighted throughout the Mass. At the beginning we pray, 'May Almighty God have mercy on us, forgive us our sins and bring us to everlasting life.' The fact that God is willing to forgive and forget all our sins (cf Heb 10:17) is mentioned repeatedly in the liturgy of the word, throughout the year. In the first eucharistic prayer we say, 'We pray to you our living and true God for our well-being and redemption.' During the consecration we proclaim, 'This is the new covenant in my blood which shall be shed for you and for all, so that sins may be forgiven.' Later, before receiving holy communion we ask, 'Lamb of God you take away the sins of the world, have mercy on us.'

Clearly, the grace of God's forgiveness flows out in a special way from Christ's wounded side in the eucharist. This awareness prompts us in words that precede the recitation of the Lord's Prayer to 'Ask our Father to forgive our sins and to bring us to forgive those who sin against us.' There are two principal reasons why it is important that this prayer be answered. Firstly, Jesus once said, 'When you are offering your gift at the altar, if you remember that your brother or sister has something against you, leave your gift there before the altar and go; first be reconciled to your brother or sister, and come and offer your gift' Mt 5:23. While God's forgiveness is abundantly *available* to us in the eucharist, we will only *experience* it to the extent that we are willing to forgive those who have offended us. 'Be merciful as God is merciful,' declared Jesus, 'judge not and you will not be judged, condemn not and you will not be condemned, forgive and you will be forgiven ... for the measure you give will be the measure you will get back' Lk 6:36-39. Secondly, it is only when we are consciously aware of God's saving grace as a result of having for-

given those who have hurt us, that we will be open to the greatness, goodness and generosity of God. It is this heartfelt awareness that evokes the inward conviction that he is willing to fulfil
his promises by granting healing to those who ask him. As the
scripture warns us, 'Does anyone harbour anger against another,
and expect healing from the Lord?' Sir 28:3.

The Eucharist and Healing

Over the years I have become increasingly convinced that
the eucharistic Jesus wants to bless those who suffer in two ways.
I have heard Sr Briege Mc Kenna say, with some justification, that
the Lord wants to offer *healing* to all, by either *helping* or *curing*
them. God can accomplish the former in two complementary
ways. Firstly, he can offer healing by helping people to see the
true spiritual meaning and purpose of the things they endure.
Speaking at Knock John Paul II articulated what they might be enabled to perceive. 'By his suffering and death Jesus took on himself all human suffering, and he gave it new value. As a matter of
fact, he calls upon the sick, upon everyone who suffers, to join
him in the salvation of the world ... This truth is very hard to
express accurately, but St Paul put it this way 'In my flesh I complete what is lacking in Christ's afflictions for the sake of his body,
that is the Church' Col 1:24.'[5] Secondly, once the Lord has revealed
truths like these, he strengthens those who suffer either in mind
or body by empowering them to bear their crosses willingly, with
patience, courage and even cheerfulness. (cf Rm 5:3-6)

In some mysterious instances Jesus in the eucharist
desires to heal some people by *curing* their mental and physical
afflictions. Why this is so, I wouldn't pretend to understand. Perhaps, all healing is a form of what theologians call 'realised escha-
tology'. In other words, the occasional cures we experience now,
are an encouraging *sign* of the total healing that will only occur
when Christ comes again in glory. What I do know is that God is
occasionally willing to cure people in Sr Briege's sense. This occurs for some of them as a result of receiving the eucharist with
expectant faith. Both our need and the Lord's willingness to heal
are often expressed in the readings, and are especially clear in the
prayers of the communion rite. From a subjective point of view,
there are certain points that I try to focus on in both. I hope that

they will not only strengthen my faith in the healing power of the eucharistic Jesus, but will also help me to encourage the same faith in the people participating in the Mass.

The Liturgy of the Word

Over the years I have discovered the relationship between the liturgy of the word, i.e. the readings and the homily, to eucharistic healing. By listening to the word of God, we get to know the God of the word. As St Jerome reminded us, 'The person who doesn't know the scriptures, doesn't know Jesus Christ,' i.e. the One who can heal us in and through the eucharist. In general terms the word of God, no matter what it's subject matter might be, can bring healing to the spirit. For example, a woman suffering from anxiety or fear might be struck by a reassuring scripture verse that evokes inner peace. As Prov 4:20-22 assures us, 'My child, pay attention to what I am telling you, listen carefully to my words; do not let them out of your sight, keep them deep in your heart, for they are *life* to those who find them and *health* to all humanity.' But needless to say, texts that refer to God's repeated promises to answer prayer, and specifically to grant healing, are particularly relevant, especially when they are backed up by scriptural examples such as the healing of the woman who suffered from chronic bleeding in Mk 5:24-35.

If the homilist *takes* the word to heart in private prayer he will be *blessed* by it. So when he comes to preach he will be in a position to *break* that word for the people in order to *give* it to them in a way that is relevant, and inspiring. (cf Lk 24:30) As St Vincent de Paul said to one of his priests, 'Let us raise our thoughts to God and be attentive to his words; one word from him is more effective and profitable than all the speculations and reasonings we can muster ... Only what is inspired by God can be profitable to us. Furthermore, we must receive from him what should be communicated to our neighbour. Thus we follow the example of Jesus who learned from his Father what he clearly spoke to the apostles and to the people who followed him' St Peter summarised this point when he wrote, 'Whoever speaks must do so as one speaking the very words of God' 1 Pt 4:11. When the exposition of God's word is backed up by examples of contemporary healing that have come to the preacher's attention, people begin to believe that 'Jesus is the same yesterday, today and forever,' Heb 13:8. They say to themselves, 'if that person was healed in that way, perhaps God will heal me too. I know that he has no favourites. We are all equally precious in his sight.'

If a listener is consciously aware of his or her needs and pays attention to God's words in the readings and homily, they can cease being nouns that are true in themselves by becoming alive and active verbs that leap with life and meaning into the heart, while evoking genuine faith. As we have noted before, 'Faith comes from hearing, and that means hearing the word of Christ' Rm 10:17. It is worth our while dwelling on this point because it is vitally important. There will be no healing without faith, and faith is evoked by the inspired and inspiring word of God.

In the Old Testament, the Hebrew for 'word' is *dabar*. It had two related meanings. It could be used as a noun to refer to the truth of the word in itself, or it could be used as a verb to refer to the truth of the word as it was addressed to a particular person or group. Used in this dynamic sense *dabar* came from a verb meaning 'to drive, to get behind and push.' 'When the Hebrew person speaks of a word,' writes a well known scripture scholar, 'he is not taking in the outside world and shaping it within himself. Rather he is thrusting something creative and powerful outward from himself into the external world and *actually changing that world* .6' (my italics) The word of God is creative, it contains within itself the Spirit given power to bring about what it says. That is why the Lord could say, 'The word that goes forth from my mouth shall not return to me empty, it shall accomplish that which I sent it to do' Is 55:11. It is this spoken word that nurtures the kind of faith that believes that whatever we ask for, believing we have received it already, will be given to us. (cf Mk 11:24)

Two Examples

Kathryn Kuhlman who had one of the most outstanding healing ministries of the century, discovered the healing power of the word early in her life. On one occasion, after she had delivered a sermon at a prayer meeting, a woman approached her and said, 'As you were preaching on the Holy Spirit, telling us that in Him lay resurrection power, I felt the Power of God flow through my body. Although not a word had been spoken regarding the healing of the sick, I knew instantly and definitely that my body had been healed. So sure was I of this, that I went to the doctor today and had my healing verified.'[7] Kathryn went on to say that this proved to be a decisive moment of revelation in her life. She recognised that the Holy Spirit was the only true healer.

A short time before, a woman rang to tell me that something similar had happened to her. She had suffered from a chronic back complaint that had failed to respond to treatment over a period of six years. Recently, this person had attended a weekend retreat, during which she had been moved and encouraged by a sermon on faith. Two days after returning home her aged sister collapsed to the floor. It was only when she bent down to assist her that she realised that her back had been completely healed. This surprised her because, apart from everything else she hadn't thought specifically about her back during the Mass. But as Jesus said, 'my words are spirit and they are life' Jn 6:63. Not only are they capable of bringing us healing, they prepare us to participate in the eucharistic prayer and to receive communion with faith and love.

The Rite of Holy Communion

The opening words of the Lord's prayer, 'Hallowed be thy name' Mt 6:9 serve as a general introduction to the theme of healing. This petition is not primarily about what we do for God, but about what God does for us in order to sanctify his name by manifesting his majesty, holiness and saving power. In Ezek 36:23 we read, 'I will hallow my great name ... and the nations will know that I am God.' 'For Jesus,' comments scripture scholar J P Meier, 'the Father reveals his transcendent holiness precisely by bringing in his eschatological kingdom, by assuming his rightful rule over the world. Hence the second petition, which we might almost translate as follows, 'Sanctify your name by bringing in your kingdom.'[8] While this petition refers primarily to the end times, it also seems to ask that God would begin to inaugurate his final victory in the here and now, not only by forgiving sins, but also by healing people as a result of either helping or curing them.

Delivered from Evil

Later in the Lord's prayer we ask the Father to 'deliver us from evil,' Mt. 6:13 i.e. to snatch us from the power of the *evil one*, i.e. Satan, though the word *ponerou* could be translated in the familiar form, as 'from evil.' In one way or another we are asking the Lord to heal us by freeing us from anything, human or non human which would try to separate us from God. As we have seen in section three, *some* of the destructive tendencies we see at work in people's lives may be due to the influence of evil spirits. For example, a person might be troubled by behaviours such as, deviant sexual compulsions, drug addiction, involvement with the occult, suicidal tendencies etc. Occasionally, problems like these are not only due to weaknesses of character and psychological problems, but to the influence of the evil spirit. John Paul II drew attention to what we have to contend with when he spoke these prophetic words at Limerick in 1979, 'Dear sons and daughters of Ireland ... your country seems to be living again the temptations of Christ ... Satan the tempter, the adversary of Christ, will use all his might and all his deceptions to win Ireland for the way of the world ... Pray, pray not to be led into temptation ... Pray that Ireland may not fail in the test. Pray as Jesus taught us to pray: 'Lead us not into temptation, but deliver us from evil'. [9]

Protection from Anxiety

Having completed the Lord's prayer we go on to pray, 'Protect us from all anxiety'. Nowadays many people lead stressful lives as a result of the pace and pressure of modern living. Indeed, it has been said with some justification that the 20th century is the 'Age of Anxiety'. In his *Introduction to the Devout Life,* St Francis de Sales writes, 'With the single exception of sin, anxiety is the greatest evil that can happen to a soul.'[10] As we saw in section two, psychologists have shown that many of our anxieties can be traced back to childhood, e.g. to a fear that we will lose the love, acceptance and approval of significant others such as parents. Because they are inclined to be mistrustful, anxious people are often self-absorbed. They tend to be defensive to a greater or lesser extent where relationships are concerned, including relationship with God. In this prayer we ask to be delivered from an inordinate desire, either to be freed from a present evil, or to acquire a hoped for good, because as St Francis suggests,[11] these are two of the principal sources of anxiety.

The Gift of Peace

Just before receiving Holy Communion we pray the following two prayers. Firstly, we say 'Lamb of God, you take away the sins of the world: grant us peace.' *Shalom* was the Old Testament word for peace. It referred to anything that enjoyed integrity, completeness and well-being. The New Testament word was *eirene*, which referred to 'the tranquil possession of good things, happiness and , *above all health*.'[12] So when we pray for peace, we ask for reconciliation with God and our neighbour, and also for health, in mind and body. Secondly, we go on to say with the Roman Centurion, 'Only say the word and I shall be healed,' (cf Mt 8:8) i.e. the alive active word, referred to above, which is capable of accomplishing what it says. Over the years I have heard people say, including a few priests, that this petition refers to spiritual healing only. Can this be true? Surely God wants to heal us as persons, i.e. in spirit, mind and body. The church resolves this apparent dilemma when it directs the celebrant to pray quietly, 'Lord Jesus Christ, with faith in your love and mercy I eat your body and drink your blood may it bring me not condemnation, but health in *mind* and *body*.'

The sentiments expressed in this prayer are confirmed by modern research. Psychosomatic medicine has shown the intimate connection between the psyche and physical health. For example it is estimated that up to seventy-five percent of all visits to doctors are made by people with stress-related problems.[13] It can be a major factor in causing high blood pressure, coronary heart disease, migraine, tension headaches, ulcers and asthmatic conditions. Researchers have discovered that while stress may be triggered by environmental conditions, usually the causes lie within. They are complex in origin. It could be that a person suffers from anxiety and insecurity because of a lack of self-acceptance, unresolved hurts in life, or repressed feelings of fear, anger, guilt, resentment etc. Such on-going attitudes and feelings of a negative kind can weaken the body's immune system thereby leaving it more vulnerable to illness and disease. For instance, in one study

Dr E M Blumberg[14] and his associates of the University of California found that in eighty-eight percent of rapidly developing and inoperable cancers, in male patients, were indirectly related to an inability to control anxiety or depression. So not surprisingly, the healing of hurting memories can be the prelude to physical healing. As one liturgical prayer puts it, 'Lord, through this sacrament may we rejoice in your healing power and experience your love in mind and body.'[15]

The Response of Faith

All we have been saying in this section comes to a focused climax, when, having heard the words, 'The body of Christ,' the person receiving the sacramental body and blood of the Lord responds, 'Amen.' A number of points came be made about this important declaration and response. Instead of distributing communion in a casual or slap dash sort of way, ministers of the eucharist, need to do so with due respect and reverence. Indeed when I am a celebrating Mass for the anointing of the sick, I momentarily raise the host and say 'The healing body of Christ,' or 'Receive the healing body of Christ'. By doing so with expectant faith, I hope to evoke a similar disposition in those receiving, one which will be encapsulated in a wholehearted acclamation of 'Amen.' This biblical word is rich in meaning. It comes from the Hebrew root *aman* which implies firmness, solidity, and a conviction that God the ever faithful One, can be relied on. Therefore, it could be translated to read, 'let it be so, I believe that it is accomplished,' or 'Yes, as a wounded person, I believe in the healing power that the Church has encouraged me to expect in this eucharist, and I am confident that it is even now being offered to me in accord with the word and the will of the Lord.' Aware, as he or she is, of the greatness, goodness and love of the Lord, the Christian's faith-filled response of , 'Amen,' is also infused with religious wonder and awe. St Cyril of Jerusalem referred to these dispositions in the fourth century, 'When you come up,' he wrote, 'to receive the Lord, make your left hand a throne for your right, the hand which is to receive the King. Receive the body of Christ in the palm of your hand and answer 'Amen'...Then, after receiving the body of Christ, go over to the chalice of his blood, Do not reach out, but bow in a gesture of adoration and veneration and answer 'Amen'.'[16]

CHAPTER 12

The Experience of Eucharistic Healing

Over the years I have come to appreciate the differing but complementary ways in which the eucharist can either maintain, improve or restore a person's health of mind and body. We can look at a few of them in turn.

Power to protect and improve one's health

A few years ago I was living in a hospital. To get to my room I had to pass through the chest ward where there were many patients suffering from smoking related ailments ranging from bronchitis to lung cancer. One day as I was saying Mass I sincerely asked the eucharistic Jesus to continue blessing me with health of mind and body. All, of a sudden an insistent question occurred to me, 'how can you ask the Lord for this gift when you insist on damaging your well-being by smoking?' I thought about this afterwards, and decided that if I was really sincere in asking for on-going good health, I'd have to give up smoking. Guided by steps one to three of A.A., I made the decision to kick the habit . Each day when I got to the prayer grant me 'health in mind and body' during Mass, I'd ask the Lord to help me. That was many years ago, I have never taken a single puff of a cigarette or cigar from that day onwards. This, I've found, is an aspect of eucharistic healing. If we are doing anything that might damage our spiritual, mental or physical health, we can rely on the Lord's help to take whatever steps are necessary to maintain or to restore it e.g. by eating less, getting more rest, taking regular exercise, giving up alcohol abuse or some other unhealthy habit, etc.

Conscious awareness of one's health needs

Beside helping to free people from negative behaviours and attitudes, the eucharist can bless them in other ways. We all come to Mass with a need for healing. It is good to consciously acknowledge one's desire for emotional and psychological help e.g. freedom from anxieties, fears and phobias, together with relief from physical ailments and disabilities e.g. arthritis, heart disease and cancer. We should allow these needs to become an aching, sighing longing prayer within us, one that reaches out to touch the hem of the Lord's eucharistic presence. Then, when we receive holy communion, Jesus can become a divine bandage wrapping himself around our woundedness. He can soak in our sin and give us his mercy, absorb our weakness and give us his strength, assimilate our brokenness and sometimes give us health of mind and body. For our part, we pray, 'If what we ask is not in accord with God's loving will or for his greater glory, grant us what is in accord with both.' In my experience eucharistic cures can come about in a number of ways.

Inner healing

Because the Mass is pre-eminently a sacrament of love that calls us to live a life of love, the celebrant may decide to assure those who are present, that if they are suffering from any inner hurt or emotional problem that would impede their ability to love, the Lord would want to heal it. Presuming people are consciously aware of some such problem, they can be encouraged to bring the painful memory or dysfunctional emotion, attitude, or compulsion to the Lord, while asking him to touch it with his healing power. Surely he would want to do so, 'Our fearlessness toward him,' therefore, 'consists in this, that if we ask anything in accordance with his will he hears us. And if we know that he listens to whatever we ask of him, we know that we already possess whatever we have asked of him' 1 Jn 5:14-15.

The Lord can cure a troubled person at communion time. For example, a few years ago I discovered that a woman attending a workshop I was conducting had been suffering from severe depression for seven or eight years. Although she had received the best of medical help, she hadn't recovered. Well, on the Saturday we celebrated the vigil Mass of Sunday. Before distributing holy communion I encouraged everyone to believe that the Lord wanted to heal those emotional problems that inhibited their ability to love. When the depressed woman came forward to receive, a lay minister of the eucharist handed her the chalice and said, 'Claire, this is the blood of Christ, may it bring you healing.' At that very moment, she became inwardly convinced that her depression was being lifted and that her hurting emotions were being healed. Immediately she began to feel better. Her recovery was rapid, complete and permanent. She hasn't suffered from depression from that day to this, and is energetically engaged in parish work ever since.

Physical Healing

Needless to say, an individual who is consciously aware of a need for physical healing can receive the eucharist with the same kind of expectant faith that led to Claire's wonderful recovery. If a celebrant is emphasising the healing dimension of the eucharist, he can take some time e.g. after the distribution of communion, to pray for various ailments. Firstly, if people have told the presiding priest about their physical problems, he can pray for them one by one, asking that they might be healed, e.g. 'we are praying for a woman who suffers from migraines ... a man with arthritis in the neck,' and so on. Secondly, he can pray for the alleviation of different physical conditions in a systematic way, beginning with the head and working downward to the feet, or visa versa, e.g. 'we are praying now for those who suffer from bad sight ... bad backs ... arthritic hips' etc. Thirdly, he can adopt a more spontaneous attitude. He would begin by asking the Lord for guidance, and continue by praying on the basis of hunches and intuitions which might occur to him in the form of images, e.g. seeing a swollen elbow in his mind's eye; or an inner 'word' about a disease like lupus, or cancer of the bowel etc. Experience teaches that while this approach to prayer can be subject to relatively harmless illusions and false inspirations, it can also be surprisingly accurate and effective.

Two Examples of Physical Healing

For example, I know a priest who had such an intuition as he prayed in Belfast on a Pentecost morning three years ago. Apparently he had a feeling there was a woman in the congregation on his left hand side, near the front of the congregation, who was suffering from tinnitus or ringing in the ears. He said a brief prayer for her, and turned his attention to other complaints. Sometime later, on a return visit to Belfast a woman approached the same priest to say that she had been present on the Pentecost Sunday. Yes, she had been a tinnitus sufferer, but thank God she had been cured. The same three approaches can be used where prayer for what is known as inner healing, or healing of memories is concerned.

More recently, a woman rang me to tell me about her eucharistic healing. She had undergone an operation to remove stones from her gall bladder. Unfortunately, the surgery had not been a great success because she continued to suffer from pain. Further investigations revealed that some of the gall stones had not been removed. Her doctor explained, 'In about two per cent of cases we fail to detect all the stones. So you still have an unresolved gall bladder problem. We will wait a while before operating on you again.' Well, sometime after receiving this bad news, the woman heard about a healing Mass that was going to be celebrated by a priest who was known to both of us. She went to the church in the expectation that she would be healed. After the distribution of communion the celebrant went to the microphone and said, 'I feel that there is a woman in the congregation who is suffering from an unresolved gall bladder problem. Believe that the Lord you received in Holy Communion, is even now healing your complaint.' Immediately, the woman felt heat going through her body as she thought, 'The priest must have been talking about me, he even repeated the very words that my doctor used.' One or two women friends, who were aware of her problem, approached her after the Mass and said, 'As soon as the priest spoke, we knew he was talking about you. The Lord must be intending to heal you.' The next day the truth of their words was underlined. The woman had no pain. Shortly afterwards she returned to the hospital for a scheduled checkup. Among other things, X-rays were taken. A week later the doctor indirectly confirmed her healing when he contacted her to say that the hospital had made a misdiagnosis after her operation. The X-rays verified the fact that there were no stones remaining in her gall bladder!

Forms of Healing Associated with the Eucharist

While the main emphasis in this chapter is on the healing power of the Mass, there are other forms of healing that can be directly or indirectly associated with it. We will look at a few.

The Rite of Anointing within Mass

Sometimes the anointing of the sick can take place within the context of Mass. It can take two forms. Firstly, there is a non-sacramental version with what is currently called, 'The oil of gladness' (cf Is 61:3).[17] Hippolytus tells us that it used to be blessed during the eucharist while saying, 'Sanctify this oil, O God, with which you anoint kings, priests and prophets, that you may grant health to those who use it and partake of it, so that it may bestow comfort on all who taste it and health on all who use it.'[18] While this oil was probably intended for use in the sacrament of the sick, Pope Innocent I, said that not only had lay people the right to be anointed by the clergy with holy oil, they could also, 'use blessed oil themselves for anointing in their own need, or in the need of members of their households.' [19]

When the priest has blessed olive oil for later use by lay people, it can be utilized during or at the end of Mass, to anoint men and women whose illnesses would not be serious enough to warrant sacramental anointing. Secondly, the sacrament itself can be administered after the liturgy of the word. It is based on a text in Jas 5:14 which reads, 'Are any among you sick? They should call for the elders of the church and have them pray over them, anointing them with oil in the name of the Lord.' In the Church's *Introduction* to the contemporary rite, par. 6, we read, 'This sacrament provides the sick person with the grace of the Holy Spirit by which the whole person is brought to health ... Thus the sick person is able not only to bear suffering bravely, but also to fight against it. A return to physical health may even follow the reception of this sacrament if it will be beneficial to the sick person's salvation.'

Happily, during parish missions we have seen all kinds of ailments being alleviated as a result of sacramental anointing administered within the context of Mass. For example, as I write I can recall a woman in Antrim and a man in Armagh who were cured of arthritis of the knees, a man in Derry City whose chronically diseased bladder recovered completely, a boy in Bellaghy whose epileptic seizures stopped altogether, a woman in Belfast whose injured shoulder and arm got better after months of pain, a woman in Lurgan whose injured spine was cured instantly, a woman in Larne whose cystitis cleared up after eight years of trouble. It gives me joy to know that Jesus who healed people in gospel times, is still giving health of mind and body to the people of our day.

Benediction with the Blessed Sacrament

Whenever I was helping to conduct parish missions, the Thursday night para-liturgical service was usually about the role of the eucharist in our lives. On a number of occasions one or other of the missioners would preach about the healing power of the sacrament. When the sermon was over the celebrant would tell the people that he was about to go among them with the monstrance. After encouraging them to reach out to the Lord with the fingers of their need, he would urge them to have confidence in the greatness, goodness and compassion of the Lord. Then he would go among the congregation. As the choir sang appropriate hymns, e.g. 'Lay your hands gently upon us,' he'd bless those who were present with the monstrance. Many people have told us how they were helped and healed by means of their faith in the Eucharistic Christ. Indeed, ever since one suicidal woman was completely cured of an emotional disorder, she has come to see me about once a year to confirm that she is still OK. More recently, a woman with a chronic back complaint felt great heat in her body as the people were blessed with the monstrance during a Thursday night mission service. Within a half an hour all her back pain had gone and happily it has not returned since then.

At the end of a healing Mass or a eucharistic service, I usually encourage the people to continue thanking God for the graces they have undoubtedly received from the Lord, either in their Spirit-given ability to endure sufferings with equanimity, or to experience a progressive recovery . One way or the other, we appreciate the gift the Lord has given us. If he has planted the seeds of a cure, our prayers of gratitude will be like refreshing rain nourishing them and enabling them to bear fruit in the future. I usually tell the members of the congregation that it is important to realise that unlike miracles, healings are not usually instantaneous. They involve a process. It is a matter of grace building on nature and that takes time – anything between a few hours and a couple of days. So unselfconsciously we praise our eucharistic Lord for the great things he is doing in our lives. We leave the outcome to his loving providence, knowing that whatever he does, 'all things work for good with those that love God' Rm 8:28.

Visits to the Blessed Sacrament

A few years ago an uncle of mine, a Jesuit in Zambia, was translating the book of Sirach into a local language, called Tonga. When he had finished a passage which contained the following verses, 'If you see an intelligent person, rise early to visit him; let your foot wear out his doorstep' Sir 6:36, he gave it to his catechist to read. Having invited his comments, he asked, 'What does that passage mean to you, from a personal point of view?' 'It is quite clear,' the man confidently replied, 'Jesus in the eucharist is the wise man, we should visit him frequently and learn from him.' While he might not have been correct from a scriptural point of view, his faith filled response reminded me of a story associated with the Curé of Ars. He had noticed that a farm labourer would leave his spade at the church door and spend hours in front of the blessed Sacrament. When he enquired how the man spent the time, he replied, 'I look at Jesus and Jesus looks at me.' It is my belief, that apart from being a contemplative activity, there is healing in that divine gaze of love.

In the quiet of a chapel, church or oratory we can silently open up our lives to the Lord. As we consciously offer him our woundedness we can do a number of things. Firstly, we can believe that in his goodness 'God strengthens us in our inner beings with power through his Spirit' Eph 3:16 and thereby affirms all that is healthy within us. Secondly, we can bless the God 'who heals us in Christ'[20] by reversing whatever might be alien to our well-being or our ability to receive and to give true Christian love. Thirdly, we could imagine that the Lord is wrapping himself, like a bandage, around our wounded humanity. As we become aware of emotional or physical hurts we can sense him drawing them out of us while giving us his healing and peace. Fourthly, we can use either of the following methods:

1. Make yourself comfortable and try to relax.

2. Make an act of faith in the eucharistic presence of Jesus. He is the same Lord who walked the roads of Galilee and who reached out in compassion to heal the sick. Notice that he looks at you with eyes filled with love and humility. He has a towel wrapped around his waist and is at at your service. Hear him say, 'What do you want me to do for you?' Mk 10:51, for in love he wants what you want. As you sense your deepest desire, the one that spontaneously emanates from your truest self, you will know what it is you really need. In all probability, it has been prompted by the Spirit at work within you. As Jesus once said, 'No one can come to me unless drawn by the Father who sent me' Jn 6:44.

3. Ask Jesus to wrap himself like a bandage around your woundedness and to pour the light of his healing power into your spirit, mind and body. You can do this in the knowledge that 'Whatever you ask for in prayer, believing that you have received it, it will be yours' Mk 11:24.

4. As you reach out with faith to touch the garment of his eucharistic presence, Imagine that God's energy, like light, is coming into your spiritual, mental, or physical hurts. Thank God that most of you is in good health and is full of life. Affirm the fact that the blueprint of wholeness which was given to you in creation, is now being restored completely by the action of the Spirit. It summons up the healing powers within your deepest self, i.e. that part of you that is in touch with God since baptism. Thank the Lord that his loving purposes are being accomplished even as you pray.

Alternative version:

1. Try to relax and make an act of faith in the presence of Jesus in the Blessed Sacrament.

2. Thank God for your good health while asking the Lord to strengthen your immune system so that it might ward of illness and disease. Even when you suffer from a problems like cancer, arthritis or angina, most of your body enjoys good health. Apart-

from your troubled parts, the rest of your body is functioning normally. You can ask the Holy Spirit to increase the well being of your healthy organs so that they will be able to influence the weaker ones in a therapeutic way.

3. Ask Jesus in the Blessed Sacrament to send you the Spirit of peace, harmony and wholeness, that it might enter the inner sanctum of every troubled cell and organ. It is good to use your imagination in this kind of prayer e.g. seeing cancer in your mind's eye as a darker area, one where there has been a rejection of the good order that regulates the workings of the rest of the body. Affirm the fact that through the action of the Holy Spirit, the Eucharistic Jesus is at work within you and that the healthy cells of the body are glowing with light and are empowered to bring the rebellious cells back into submission. You could imagine the healthy cells carrying flags marked with the sign of the cross. They do battle and rejoice as they win victory after victory in the name of the Lord. You can say to Jesus, 'I thank you, Lord of light, that you are banishing the darkness in my body by the power of your Spirit at work within me. Where there is disease i.e. lack of ease, you are giving me, ease i.e. peace, harmony and wholeness.'

4. If you need inner healing, you can offer your psyche or mind to the Lord who is present in the Blessed Sacrament while asking him to fill your thoughts, feelings, attitudes, memories unconscious etc. with his healing Spirit. Because they can sometimes be a block to to the Spirit ask the Lord to bring to mind anything that he would want to deal with. You may find that negative feelings, like fear, anger, resentment together with forgotten memories begin to surface. As you allow yourself to re-experience them, share them prayerfully with the Lord. Ask him to pour his healing Spirit into them in the belief that it can 'Destroy false arguments and pull down every proud obstacle raised against the knowledge of God by taking every thought captive by bringing it into obedience to Christ' 2 Cor 10:5-7. If you are aware of resentments the Spirit will not only prompt you you to forgive those who have hurt you in the past, it will empower you to do so as well. This is the indispensable key that opens the psyche to all kinds of inner healing.

5. If you have reason to suspect that the evil spirit is impinging upon your inner life in a disturbing way, you can feel sure in the

presence of Jesus in the blessed sacrament that he will give you the authority in his name to pray against it e.g. 'The Lord, delivers me from all evil, and I say to you unclean spirit ... (you might be able to say what kind of spirit it is e.g. spirit of the occult ... destructive spirit etc.) depart from my life, I don't want to have anything to do with you. And now Lord I invite you to fill me with your Holy Spirit, to guide me in all things and to preserve me now and in the future from all illusions and false inspirations. Amen.'

CHAPTER 13

The Eucharist as Symbol of Transformation

In the eucharist, bread and wine which have been made from wheat and grapes, representative fruits of the earth, are offered to the Lord. At the consecration, the priest asks the Spirit of God to fall upon them, in order to transform them into the sacramental body, and blood, of Christ. Implicit in that prayer is a secondary invocation that, 'we may come to share in the divinity of Christ, who humbled himself to share in our humanity.' Like Lucy, the woman mentioned earlier, we long for an outpouring of that same Holy Spirit which can sanctify and make all things new. This can occur as we receive the eucharist which is both the sign, source and goal of our gradual divinization.[21] As one document put it, 'In this Sacrament of bread and wine, of food and drink, everything that is human really undergoes a singular transformation and elevation.'[22] In a word, we aim to become what we eat. This notion of personal transformation, as symbolized by the eucharist, is implicit in a number of scripture passages. For example in Rm 12:2 we read, 'Do not model your behaviour on the contemporary world, but let the renewing of your minds transform you.' The author of Eph 4:22-24 says, 'Put aside your old self, which belongs to your old way of life and is corrupted by following illusory desires. Your mind must be renewed in spirit so that you can put on the new man that has been created on God's principles, in the uprightness and holiness of the truth.' Finally, Col 3:10 observes, 'You have stripped off your old behaviour with your old self, and you have put on a new self which will progress towards true knowledge the more it is renewed in the image of its Creator.'

Traditional Christian spirituality has described how, following a genuine spiritual awakening, a disciple of the Lord can expect to embark on a three stage journey of inner transformation.[23] During the purgative period he or she learns to renounce sins, bad habits, addictions and worldly attachments. According to Carmelite spirituality, this is the time during which the external

174

and internal senses are purified i.e. the capacity for external bodily pleasure, and the inner pleasures of the imagination and memory. The emotions, intellect and will are cleansed of anything that could be a barrier to union with God. During the illuminative stage, a man or woman is interiorly enlightened concerning things of the spirit. When the unitive stage is reached, he or she enjoys a sense of direct rapport with God through mystical union with the person of Christ. I may say in passing, that although these stages are sequential, they also overlap insofar as elements from the purgative and illuminative stages may appear in the unitive state, and visa versa. As a result of undergoing this kind of Exodus experience, by passing from slavery to sinful human desires to the freedom of the children of God, a person can become holy as God is holy (cf 1 Pt 1:16).

In recent years a growing number of psychologists such as Jung,[24] Assagioli,[25] and May[26] have indicated how there is a relationship between spiritual holiness and psychological wholeness. They have also described the possible dynamics of such psycho-spiritual development. By and large they seem to agree that the person has to achieve, what they variously refer to as individuation, super consciousness, or transcendence, by moving from the limitations of the egocentric ego to get in touch with the true self. At its deepest level it is anchored in the mystery of the Holy One who upholds and fulfils it. Jung claimed that the Alchemists of old had indirectly tried to describe this unconscious process of transformation. For example, they looked for a way in which a mixture of mercury, sulphur and salt could be transmuted into gold. According to Jung, this was really a material symbol for a deep-seated desire for psycho-spiritual transformation.[27] It always involves a painful process of letting go of egotism in order to become more open to the deeper self as it progressively finds it's fulfilment through conscious relationship to the Beyond in whom 'we live and move and have our being' Acts 17:28.

In many of his writings he outlined the ways in which this Paschal process of dying and rising, which is depicted in the eucharistic sacrifice, might occur during painful life crises e.g. through the archetypal activity of the personal and collective unconscious which is often revealed in dreams. This dynamic, he writes, 'is likewise expressed in Christian Dogma and more particularly in the transformation symbolism of the Mass. The psychology of this process makes it easier to understand why in the Mass man appears as both the sacrificer and the sacrificed gift, and why it is not man who is these things, but God who is in both, why God becomes the suffering and dying man, and why man, through partaking of the glorified body, gains the assurance of resurrection and becomes aware of his participation in Godhead.'[28] This is a difficult subject.[29] Suffice it to say, that Jung has shown how the contemporary desire for psycho-spiritual healing and integration through contact with the mystery of God can be facilitated by the profound transformation symbolism of the Mass and faith-full reception of Holy Communion. As an individual attains wholeness in this way, he or she is empowered to transform society by removing obstacles to unity and peace.

The Eucharist and the Healing of Society

Earlier it was suggested that as God's bandage the eucharistic Jesus wraps himself around our wounded humanity in order to bring us not only mercy but also healing of mind and body. During the consecration he says to his disciples, 'Do this in memory of me.' Not only is he instructing us to re-enact his loving sacrifice in a sacramental way, he is also urging us to love one another just as he has loved us. The celebrant has this in mind when, at the end of the eucharist, he dismisses the people with the words, 'The Mass is ended let us go in peace, to love and serve the Lord,' i.e. in the person of our wounded neighbours. As St Vincent de Paul once pointed out, it is simply a matter of 'leaving God for God.'[30]

Among other things, we are called to become Christ's poultice, by enfolding the woundedness of others with his/our gentleness and compassion. If we are willing to listen to the 'still sad music of humanity' and to respond to it in a practical way, we will be able to comfort and heal others in their afflictions, with the comfort and healing we ourselves have received from God in and through the eucharist (cf 2 Cor 1:4). Like the Good Samaritan we will be able to bandage people's wounds by metaphorically pouring oil and wine upon them (cf Lk 10:33). There are a number of ways in which this can be done. However we will mention only three, by striving for ecumenical reconciliation, praying for the healing of others and working to overcome all those forms of injustice which oppress people and directly or indirectly hurts them in mind or body.

Ecumenical Reconciliation

At the last supper Jesus prayed, 'I pray not only for these but also for those who through their teaching will come to believe in me. May they all be one, just as, Father, you are in me and I am in you, so that they also may be in us, so that the world may believe it was you who sent me' Jn 17:21. St Paul echoed this prayer when he said, 'I appeal to you, make my joy complete by being of a single mind, one in love, one in heart and one in mind.' He then goes on to show how this could be achieved by imitating the self-emptying Christ of the eucharist, 'Nothing is to be done,' he says, 'out of jealousy or vanity; instead out of humility of mind everyone should give preference to others, everyone pursuing not selfish interests but those of others' Phil 2:2-5. While these sentiments should inform community life within all the churches, they should also inform ecumenical contacts between the churches. As the Rev Cecil Kerr, of the Christian Renewal Centre in Rostrevor, has said repeatedly, 'there is no genuine renewal without reconciliation.' When he visited Ireland in 1979, Pope John Paul II pointed to the connection between renewal within and between the churches. 'Renewal is itself an indispensable contribution to the work of unity between Christians ... In our search for holiness and for authentic Christian living, we shall be coming closer to Christ, and therefore closer to one another in Christ. It is he alone, through the action of the Holy Spirit, who can bring our hopes to fulfilment.'[31] That said, we need to take as many practical steps as we can to build bridges of understanding and cooperation so the day will come when we can share the eucharist as the sign of the ecclesial unity already achieved.

A few years ago I attended an ecumenical prayer meeting in the North of Ireland, during which the Lord led me into an understanding of the relationship between the cross and reconciliation. In my mind's eye I could see a number of tall flagpoles with their respective flags flapping in the wind. At the base of each flagpole were groups of men and women. They were shouting and angrily gesticulating at the people gathered around the other flagpoles. Then, in the middle, I beheld the cross. At first the people didn't even see it, they were so preoccupied by their own disputes. Then, one by one, the angry protesters began to pay attention to the crucified One. As they beheld him, their indignation turned to shame. Each group began to lower its flag, some slowly, others more rapidly. Soon the cross stood higher than all the flags. People began to drift away from their flagpoles to gather around the foot of the cross. It seemed as if the Lord were saying, 'At the moment the flags and emblems of your denominational, nationalistic and community pride are raised higher than the cross. But when you learn to look to him who was lifted up from the earth to draw all people to himself, you will lower the flags of your pride. Then, and only then, will you find peace. For in the power of the cross, the dividing walls of your divisions will crumble.'

Already a great deal has happened. For example, I was greatly honoured some time ago when I was invited, with official approval, to be the first Catholic priest since the Reformation, to say Mass for an ecumenical gathering in Brecon Cathedral, in Wales. Since then I have conducted a mission in a modern Church in Warrington, in England, which is jointly owned and used by the local Catholics and Anglicans. I have also ministered in a parish in the West of Ireland, where a collection was being held in order to help to defray the heavy expense of repairing the local Protestant church. Although, a great deal remains to be done, we can only thank God that we have already come a long way since the time before the Second Vatican Council.

Praying for the Healing of Others

Although Jesus commissioned his followers to heal the sick, (cf Mk 16:18) until recently, this aspect of Christ's ministry was largely ignored in the official teaching and liturgy of the Church.[32] The second Vatican Council redressed this imbalance, principally by revising the liturgy of anointing. Instead of administering 'extreme unction' in order to bring spiritual healing to those who were about to die, it stated that 'the sacrament of the sick' could be administered to anyone who had a life threatening illness in order to bring the person healing of mind and body. It is

my hope that increasing numbers of the clergy will compassion-
ately offer sacramental anointing in the firm expectation that it
will bring them healing, either in the form of comfort or cure. As
St James says, 'Anyone of you who is ill should send for the elders
of the church (i.e. ordained priests) and they must anoint the sick
person with oil in the name of the Lord and pray over the person.
The prayer of faith will save the sick person ... Pray for one another, *so
that you may be healed.* The prayer of the righteous is powerful and
effective.' Jas 5:14-16.

Vatican II also indicated in par. 12 of *The Constitution on
the Church* and par, 3 of *The Constitution on the Laity*, how any baptised person could participate in the healing ministry of Christ. 'It
is not only through the sacraments and Church ministries that the
Holy Spirit sanctifies and leads the people of God and enriches it
in virtues[33] ... The Spirit of the Lord gives a vast variety of charisms (including that of healing) inviting people to assume different ministries and forms of service, and reminding them, as he reminds all people in their relationship in the Church, that what
distinguishes persons is not an increase in dignity, but a special
and complementary capacity for service.'[34] A number of points
can be made in this connection. Firstly, the service we offer people
through the charismatic ministry of healing is an expression of the
kind of mercy and compassion poured out upon us in the eucharist. Secondly, it would appear that only those who have been
'baptised in the Spirit,'[35] are graced with the charisms which are
mentioned by St Paul in 1 Cor 12:4-11. Thirdly, only a minority of
those who receive the fulness of the Spirit are specifically graced
with the gift of healing. Paul asks in a rhetorical way, 'Do all possess gifts of healing?' in 1 Cor 12:30. His answer is 'no,' the gift of
healing, like the others is only given to some Christians for the
sake of the many who are members, or potential members of
Christ's body, the Church. So, all of us lay people and clergy alike
can earnestly desire to be 'filled with the Spirit' Eph 5:18, and 'to
receive the gifts of the Spirit,' 1 Cor 14:1, including the charism of
healing. We do so in order that we might demonstrate in deeds of
power, the divine love proclaimed in the gospel.

In recent years, many Catholics have rediscovered the rite
of non-sacramental anointing[36] with the 'oil of gladness' which is

provided for in the Roman Ritual.[37] A prayer is said by a priest over some olive oil. It includes the words, 'Let it bring health in body and mind to all who use it ... You have ordained it for the anointing the sick, so that, when they are made well, they may give thanks to you, the Living and true God.' While only a few men and women receive the charism of healing, the oil of gladness can be used with prudence by any believing and compassionate Christian. Instead of praying with the charism of faith, that a suffering brother or sister might be healed, a person can pray with trusting faith that the sufferer will recover in accordance with the promises of Christ. I know many lay people who bring a small container of the oil with them wherever they go. If a family member, friend or workmate is ailing, they may discretely offer to anoint him or her with the sign of the cross, while saying something like the following, 'Through this holy anointing, may the Lord in his love, heal you in spirit, mind and body, in the name of the Father, and of the Son, and of the Holy Spirit. Amen.' Repeatedly, I have heard wonderful accounts of how such prayerful anointings have proved effective.

Opposing Injustice and Oppression

Over the years I have noticed something, which has been confirmed time and time again by researchers of different kinds. Social injustice hurts and wounds both individuals and communities. As a result their self-esteem is lowered, their potential retarded, their hopes disappointed and their ability to love tenderly, inhibited. If we wish to be for others, what Christ has been for us in the eucharist, i.e. a healing remedy for mind and body, we need to identify, and oppose those forms of injustice and oppression which tend to diminish people. For example, a few years ago I met an interesting widow in North County Dublin. She told me how one Thursday morning after the ten Mass, she was driving through her town. The day was windy, wet and cold. As she passed the local welfare office, she noticed a long queue of unemployed people, young and old alike, waiting outside to get their benefits. Her heart went out to these men and women, some of whom were known to her. She felt compassion when she noticed how they had to endure such miserable and humiliating circumstances. As she reflected on what she had seen, she sensed anger and indignation welling up inside her. Her feelings found expression in a letter she wrote later that day to a local newspaper, in which she proposed two practical changes. Firstly, if a parish hall which happened to be near the welfare office, were made available when necessary, it could protect people from the elements and the curious gaze of the public. Secondly, she proposed that welfare benefits could be given out two days a week. This would help to half the queues. In the event, a local politician, another woman, saw the letter, was moved by it, investigated the situation and had some of the widow's suggestions implemented. By engaging in any kind of action for justice, a person can bring the liberating and healing love of the eucharistic Jesus into the marketplace of people's everyday struggles.[38]

The Eucharist and the Healing of Nature

In recent years, science has increasingly stressed the fact that all creation is one, and that everything that exists from the most gigantic galaxy to the minutest sub atomic particle is interconnected. Theorists like David Bohm talk about the holographic universe, one in which each part is in the whole and the whole is in each part. This notion is evident in biology. Apparently the entire genetic code of the human body is present in each and every one of its billions of cells. In theory an identical person could be cloned from a single cell taken from either the body of a man or woman. This holistic principle has always been familiar to contemplatives both East and West. For example a Buddhist sutra states, 'In heaven there is said to be a network of pearls so arranged that if you look at one you see all the others reflected in it. In the same way, each object in the world is not merely itself but involves every other object, and in fact *is* every other object.'[39] In the West, William Blake bore witness to the same kind of unitary awareness when he wrote, 'Five windows light the caverned man, and if these windows are cleansed the result is that everything is seen as it really is, infinite.' In his *Auguries of Innocence*, he described the contemplative's ability 'To see a world in a grain of sand and a heaven in a wild flower, hold infinity in the palm of your hand and eternity in an hour.'

In the eucharist, the bread and wine are made from wheat

and grapes, representative fruits of the material world. At the consecration the Holy Spirit falls upon them and transforms them into the real but sacramental presence of Jesus Christ. This occurs by means of what theologians refer to as transubstantiation. It is an amazing miracle. Mere matter, the work of human hands, becomes the locus of the divine presence. But in the light of an holistic perspective, the implications are momentous. If God is present in part of the material world, surely his fiery finger has been plunged in a qualified sense into the heart of the entire material universe. The late Teilhard de Chardin has explored the possible relationship between the eucharist and the elan, both of human and evolutionary development.[40] In a very real way, it is 'charged with the grandeur of God.' A few years ago I tried to capture this awareness in the following words, 'Silent sound of Spirit wings, beating in the heart of everything, world aglow, flesh of God, hidden Host of all that is.'

It seems to me, that this perspective leads to two important consequences. Firstly, those who discern the presence of Christ in the eucharist, should also realise that instead of being a dead, inert thing, to be ruthlessly exploited, all nature is holy, the dwelling place of the One who is Immanuel, God with us. As such it should be reverenced, protected and wherever possible, repaired and restored. Those who receive Christ in the eucharist are in a position therefore, to provide the ecological movement with a spiritual basis for the all important task of trying to heal the many wounds that have been inflicted on mother nature. After all, we need her even more than she needs us. This leads us to our second consequence. From nature's bounty we derive all the chemicals used in modern medicine. As Sir 38:4;7 reminds us, 'The Lord has brought forth medicinal herbs from the ground, and no one sensible will despise them ... He uses these for healing and relieving pain; the chemist makes up a mixture from them.' In other words there is a link between the eucharist and the healing efforts of the pharmaceutical industry and indeed of the entire medical profession who use them.

Conclusion

As the church rediscovers the healing power of the sacraments,[41] especially the anointing of the sick and the eucharist, it will add credibility to its proclamation of the gospel by answering a deep-seated need in God's people. As Frank Mc Nutt once wrote, 'If we preach the power of Jesus to save and redeem the whole person, people want to see that power made real.'[42] I'm sure that it is a good and worthwhile thing for Catholics to go to places like Lourdes and San Giovanni Rotondo. Thank God many of us will have heard of someone who was healed in one or other of those places of pilgrimage.

That said, Frank O' Connor translated a poem from the Irish which says, 'To go to Rome is little profit endless pain, the master you seek in Rome, you find at home, or seek in vain.'[43] I dream that a day will come when Catholics won't necessarily have to go to far away places in search of a cure. All they will have to do is to attend Mass in their local church in order to experience the healing power of the Lord. If prayers like these from the liturgy of anointing are offered with sincerity and faith anything could happen. 'Through your gift of the Spirit, you bless us, even now, with comfort and healing, strength and hope, forgiveness and peace ... Father accept this offering from your whole family, and especially those who ask for healing of body, mind and spirit. Grant us peace in this life, save us from final damnation, and count us among those you have chosen.' As prayers like these are answered, perhaps we will get used to seeing such things as crutches, spectacles and hearing aids hanging on the walls of our churches as tangible reminders of the great things the Lord has done in accordance with his promises! As far as I can now remember Coventry Patmore once wrote, 'We are wrapped and swathed round in dreams, dreams that are enigmatical, and the future comes not true, save through these.'

Notes

INTRODUCTION

1. 'Faith, Science and the Search for Truth,' *Origins*, Washington D.C. 1979, p. 390.
2. Ed. J Murphy, Columba, Dublin, 1992, pp. 40-66.
3. Ed. P Waldron, Pub. St John's College Waterford, pp. 19-25.
4. *The Pastoral Rule*, Bk. 2, 4. Office of readings, week 27 of *The Divine Office*. p. 609.
5. Of Studies, *Essays*, J M Dents& Sons Ltd. London, 1972, p.150.
6. Quoted from St Thomas Aquinas in *A New Catechism*, Burns & Oates, London, 1967, p. 33.

PART 1: LIVING THE MYSTERY OF FAITH

1. *Dynamics of Faith*, (N.Y. Harper & Row, 1957.) p1.
2. *L'Action* 1893, cf. H Bouillard, *The Logic of the Faith*, (Gill & Son, Dublin, 1967), pp. 161-181.
3. *Faith and Doctrine*, Newman Press, NY. 1969.
4. *A Rumor of Angels: Modern Society and a Rediscovery of the Supernatural*, Pelican, 1970, London.
5. *Two Types of Faith*, (N.Y. Harper & Row, 1961.)
6. *Faith and Belief*, Princeton, (N.J. 1979.)
7. *Stages of Faith*, (San Francisco, Harper & Row, 1981.)
8. 'The Absence of God in Modern Culture' in *Second Collection*, Ed. Ryan & Tyrell, (Philadelphia, The Westminster Press, 1974) pp. 101-116.
9. Karl Rahner augmented this point when he said, 'Our present situation is one of transition from a Church sustained by a homogeneous Christian society and almost identical with it, from a people's Church, to a Church made up of those who have struggled against the environment in order to reach a clear personal and explicitly responsible decision of faith.' *The Practice of Faith: A Handbook of Contemporary Spirituality*, SCM Press, London, 1985, p 30.
10. *Belonging to the Universe: New Thinking about God and Nature*, Penguin, London, 1992, pp. xi - xv. *c.f.* Diarmuid Ó Murchú, *Our World in Transi-*

tion: Making Sense of a Changing World, Temple House Books, Sussex, 1992, for an interesting survey of some on the paradigms mentioned in the first book.

11. *The Faith that Does Justice*, Ed. J. C. Haughey, (N.Y. Paulist Press, 1972.)

12. Hodgson, *New Birth of Freedom*, Fortress, Philadelphia, 1976, p. 333.

13. In his *Apostolic Preaching and its Development*, and *The Essential Nature of New Testament Preaching*, C H Dodd maintains that an examination of 1 Cor 15 and the speeches in Acts shows that the kerygma normally contained the following six points.

1. The age of fulfilment has dawned: the Old Testament prophesies have been realised; the hope of Israel is now present in fact.

2. This fulfilment is shown by the life, death and resurrection of Jesus the Messiah.

3. In virtue of the resurrection he is exalted as Lord.

4. The Holy Spirit's presence in the church is a token of God's favour toward his people.

5. Christ will come again as Judge and Saviour.

6. There is an appeal for repentance, an offer of forgiveness and the gift of the Holy Spirit, and an assurance of salvation.

14. *Maturing in the Spirit*, (Dublin, Columba, 1991), pp. 34-36.

15. General audience Nov 8th. 1978.

16. 'Spirituality of the Future,' in *The Practice of Faith: A Handbook of Contemporary Spirituality*, SCM, London, 1985, p. 22.*c.f.* 'The Contemplative Dimension of Religious Life,' Flannery (ed), *Vatican Council II*, Dominican Publications, Dublin, 1982, p. 258.

17. Billy Graham, 'The Holy Spirit and Salvation,' in *The Holy Spirit*, (London, Fount, 1980), pp. 59-60.

18. *The Call to Conversion*, Lion, (Herts., Lion, 1986), esp. pp. 18-38.

19. *Decree on Justification* (1547) chap. VI. in Neuner and Dupuis (eds) *The Christian Faith*, Mercier, Dublin & Cork, 1972, (no. 1929.)

20. Decree on Justification, chap. IX. op. cit. (no. 1936.)

21. *c.f.* Code of Canon Law, No. 849.

22. P. Coste, ed, *Saint Vincent de Paul: Correspondence, Entretiens, Documents* Vol. XI 342.

23. *Evangelization Today*, Par. 75.

24. *Christian Initiation and Baptism in the Holy Spirit: Evidence from the First Eight Centuries*, Liturgical Press, Collegeville, 1991, p. 337.

25. See P. Collins, 'Forgiveness and Healing' in *Growing in Health and Grace*, (Galway, Campus 1991.)

26. *Growing in Health and Grace*, op. cit., 1991, pp. 14-16, 40-41.

27. Quoted by Bernard Bro in *The Little Way: The Spirituality of Thérèse of Lisieux*, DLT, London, 1979, p. 66.

Rightly or wrongly the approach of Thérèse seems to me to be similar to that of Luther whose central intuition, 'ruled out every attempt to justify or acquit oneself before God. One was made acceptable or justified before God in faith, that is, in the lively apprehension of God's word of love and mercy. Before God, this alone was the ground of trust.' John Dillenberger, (ed.) *Martin Luther: Selections*, Doubleday Anchor, 1961, p. xxvi.

For example, Luther wrote these striking words in 1521 in a letter to Melanchthon, 'Be a sinner and sin boldly, but believe still more boldly and rejoice in Christ, who is victor over sin, death and the world. Sin we must, as long as we live here ...It is enough that we recognize, through the riches of the glory of God, the Lamb who takes away the sins of the world. From him no sin will sever us, even though we should fornicate or commit murder a million times a day. Do you think that the price or ransom of our sins in this Lamb was so small?'

28. See P. Collins, 'Be guided by the Spirit' in *Maturing in the Spirit*.

29. Cecil Kerr, *The Way of Peace: Peace Amidst the Conflict of Northern Ireland* (London, Hodder & Stoughton, 1990.) Gemma Costello, *In God's Hands: A Story of Sr Consilio and Cuan Mhuire* (Dublin, Veritas, 1985.)

30. *Only One Earth* (London, Pelican, 1972) p.35

31. General Audience, 6th. Sept. 1978.

32. For more on this subject see section three below.

33. *Eternal Life* (London, Fount, 1985), p. 167.

34. J. Mc Manus, 'Exorcism in Catholic Moral Theology' in *Deliverance Prayer*, Ed. M & D Linn, (N.Y. Paulist Press, 1981), pp. 242-251.

35. *Code of Canon Law*, 1172 .1

36. For more on this see, P Collins, 'Exorcism and the Falling Phenomenon' in *Maturing in the Spirit*, chap. 10.

37. *Contra Fabianum*, Fragment 28; PL 65, 791.

38. Abbott, 'The Church', *Documents of Vat. II*, par 12.

39. E. D. O' Connor, Ed. *Pope Paul and the Spirit*, (Notre Dame, Ave Maria Press, 1978.)

40. Cat 5, 10-11, Readings, week 31, Wed., *The Divine Office* Vol. 3.

41. *c.f.* 'Healing and the Priesthood' by Frank Mc Nutt, *New Covenant*, (Nov. 1979.)

42. *Jesus of Nazareth* , (N.Y. Harper & Row, 1930), p. 131

43. *Rediscovering the Teaching of Jesus*, (N.Y. Harper & Row, 1967), p. 15.

44. 'Faith' in *A glimpse into Glory*, Logos (N.J. Logos, 1979), p. 45.

45. 'Faith vs. Hope' in *Faith to Live By* (Ann Arbor, CGM/Servant, 1977), p. 23.

46. 'Be Guided by the Spirit' in *Maturing in the Spirit*, 1990, and 'Praying for Healing' sec. 3. pp. 96-112 & 130-134.

47. *Christian Initiation and Baptism in the Holy Spirit*, op. cit. p. 337.

48. For more on this point see the section on 'The Liturgy of the Word' in chapter eleven below.

49. Pub. Lakeland, London, 1967.

50. Lakeland, London, 1963.

51. Lakeland, London.

52. Oliphants, London, 1974.

53. Ed. Jamie Buckingham, Logos, N.J. 1979.

54. Jamie Buckingham, Logos, N.J.1978.

55. Simi & Segreti, Tan, Rockford, 1977.

56. *Scale of Perfection*, 2.25 Tr. G. Sitwell, Burns Oates, London, 1953, p 209.

57. Quoted by K Leech in *True God*, Sheldon Press, London, 1985, p 5.

58. *Contemplative Prayer*, DLT, London, 1973, pp 96-97.

59. A Jewish author named Richard Rubenstein has claimed that the experience of the holocaust has had a significant effect on theology. 'The time of the death of God does not mean the end of all gods. It means the demise of the God who was the ultimate actor in history. I believe in God the Holy Nothingness, known to mystics of all ages, out of which we have come, and to which we shall ultimately return.' *After Auschwitz: Radical Theology and Contemporary Judaism*, Bobs-Merrill, Indianapolis, 1966, p 154.

60. Cat. 5-10, op. cit.

61. *Power Evangelism*, (London, Hodder & Stoughton, 1985), and *Power Healing*, (London, Hodder & Stoughton, 1986.)

PART 2: FAITH AND PROTECTION FROM ANXIETY

1. Cf B Lonergan, 'Feelings' Part 1, chap. 2, sec. 3, *Method in Theology*, DLT, London, 1972, pp 30-34. J Macquarrie, 'Feeling' chap. 8, *Existentialism*, Penguin, London, 1973, pp 118-134. P Collins, 'Fingerprints of the Heart' Part 1, chap. 3, *Intimacy and the Hungers of the Heart*, Columba, Dublin 1991, pp 43-58.

2. *Fallible Man*, p. 161.

3. *Clinical Theology*, DLT, London, 1986, p. 39.

4. Karl Rahner has written: 'The human person's first personal partner in terms of his categorical life, cannot be God, because a mediation is always needed. Because of the historicity and factitiousness of the human situation, then, the human person and the world must be the mediator.' 'Reflections on the unity of the love of neighbour and the love of God', *Theological Investigations*, Vol 6, London, DLT, 1969, p 241

5. Book three, 'The Mad Man' in *The Gay Science*.

6. *Transpersonal Development*, Crucible, London, 1991, p. 29.

7. *Transpersonal Development*, op. cit. p. 169.

8. *Janus: A Summing Up*, Pan/Picador, London, 1979, p 1.

9. *The Denial of Death*, Free Press, N.Y. 1973.

10. *On Death and Dying*, Tavistock Publications, London, 1973.

11. From *Collected Works*, Weimar edn., vol 37:661, 20. as quoted in *The Common Catechism*, Search Press London, 1975, p. 38.

12. Wendy Wright has written, 'While a student at Paris he had been terror struck at the doctrine of predestination that the theological masters Augustine of Hipo and Thomas Aquinas had formulated in early centuries. According to the revered doctors, God had predestined certain individuals to be the elect and one had actually no sort of assurance beyond faith that one might be one of the chosen number.' *Bond of Perfection*, Paulist Press, N.J. 1985, p. 59.

13. *Bond of Perfection*, op. cit. p 59.

14. Nowadays we tend to treat scrupulosity as a psychological rather than a spiritual problem. Clinically, it would be diagnosed as an obsessional compulsive neurosis and treated as such.

15. *The Autobiography of St Ignatius Loyola*, Harper Torchbooks, NY, 1974, p. 35.

16. *The Autobiography*, op. cit. p 36.

17. *c.f.* P Collins, *Intimacy and the Hungers of the Heart*, op. cit. pp. 181-184.

18. *Intimacy*, op. cit. pp. 146-149.

19. Quoted by Henri Troyat in *Tolstoy*, Pelican Biographies, London, 1970, p. 520.

20. Troyat, op. cit. p. 520.

21. *Confessions* quoted by Troyat, op cit. p. 521.

22. *Confessions* quoted by Troyat, op. cit. p. 524.

23. *Autobiography of a Saint*, The Harvill Press,, London, 1958, p. 255-256.

24. Quoted by Bernard Bro in *The Little Way: The Spirituality of Thérèse of Lisieux*, DLT, London, 1979, p. 11.

25. Quoted by D A Flemming (ed) in *The Fire and the Cloud: An Anthology of Catholic Spirituality*, Geoffrey Chapman, London, 1978, pp. 309-310.

26. Burnt Norton, in *Four Quartets*, Faber, London, p. 14.

27. *The World is too Much with Us*, line 1.

28. Tom and Pat Malone, *The Art of Intimacy*, Simon & Schuster, London, 1987, p. 28.

29. Paul Tillich, *The Courage to Be*, Fontana, London, 1962, p. 71.

30. C. G. Jung, 'Psychotherapists or the Clergy,' in *Psychology and Western Religion*, Arc, London, 1988, p. 208.

31. *c.f.* Mt 5:3 'Blessed are the poor in Spirit, for theirs is the kingdom of heaven.'

32. A favourite phrase of St Thérèse of Lisieux, based on the text 'Unless

you become as little children, you shall not enter the kingdom of God.' Lk 18:29.

33. Quoted by John Macquarrie in *Jesus Christ in Modern Thought*, SCM, London, 1990, p. 197.

34. Quoted by L Boros in *Meeting God in Man*, Burns & Oates, London, 1968, p. 91.

35. *Psychology and Western Religion*, Arc, London, 1988, p. 212.

36. 'The Experience of Theophanies,' in *Heightened Consciousness: The Mystical Difference*, Paulist Press, N.Y. 1991, pp. 35-36.

37. *Man's Search for Meaning*, Hodder & Stoughton, London, 1962.

38. 'Man's Approach to God' in *A Maritain Reader*, (ed Gallagher & Gallagher) Image, NY, 1966, p. 96-97.

39. *c.f.* J Hick, *An Interpretation of Religion*, Macmillan, London, 1989, pp. 75-79.

40. *c.f.* T Mc Dermott (ed) *Summa Theologiae: A concise Translation*, Methuen, London, 1989, pp. 12-14.

41. *A Maritain Reader*, op. cit. p. 97.

42. The numinous refers to a non-rational and amoral kind of religious experience of the 'holy'. The numinous includes feelings of awe and self-abasement as well as an element of religious fascination.

43. Cardinal Newman's distinction in *An Essay in Aid of a Grammar of Assent*, Longmans, London, 1903, chap. IV, sec. 2. Speaking of real assents he says, 'They are sometimes called beliefs, convictions, certitudes ... they are perhaps as rare as they are powerful. Till we have them ... we have no intellectual moorings.'

44. *Daily Mail*, Mon 25 April 1955.

45. *The Shaking of the Foundations*, Penguin, London, 1966, pp. 163-164.

46. *c.f.* P Collins, *Intimacy and the Hungers of the Heart*, op. cit pp. 180-184.

47. *Intimacy*, op. cit. pp. 184-187 & 199-205.

48. c.f. *Summa Theologiae: A concise Translation*, op. cit. pp. 110-111.

49. *The Range of Reason*, Geoffrey Bless Ltd. London, 1953, p. 60.

50. *Philosophy of Religion*, Prentice-Hall Inc., NJ, 1990, p. 125-129.

51. *c.f.* P. Collins, *Maturing in the Spirit*, Columba, Dublin, 1991, pp. 109-110.

52. Corgi, London, 1977.

53. *c.f.* P Collins, 'Overcoming Stress' in *Growing in Health and Grace*, Campus, Galway, 1991, pp. 44-72.

54. Cardinal Newman, *Lead Kindly Light*.

55. 'The Two Standards' in *Meditations on Priestly Life*, Sheed & Ward, London, 1970, p. 174.

56. c.f. Jim Wallis, *The Call to Conversion*, Lion, London, 1981.

57. Fontana Books, London, 1966, p. 172.

58. *Becoming Adult Becoming Christian*, Harper & Row, San Francisco, 1984, p. 70

59. Marghanita Laski, *Ecstasy*, Cresset, London, 1961.

60. Adam Curle, *Mystics and Militants*, Tavistock, London, 1972.

61. Abraham Maslow, *Religions, Values, and Peak-Experiences*, Ohio State University, Ohio, 1964.

62. *Transpersonal Development*, op. cit. p. 29.

63. *Psychology and Western Religion*, op. cit. p. 202. 'Among all my patients in the second half of life – that is to say, over thirty-five – there has not been one whose problem in the last resort was not that of finding a religious outlook on life. It is safe to say that every one of them fell ill because he had lost that which the living religions of every age have given to their followers, and none of them was really healed who did not regain his religious outlook.'

64. 'The Origin and Development of personal identity through childhood to adult life: and its significance in pastoral care.' Second year syllabus, no. 4, *Clinical Theology*, (The Clinical Theological Assn. Hawthornes of Nottingham Ltd.) p. 5.

65. *Clinical Theology* op. cit. p. 101.

66. *Clinical Theology*, op. cit. p. 13.

67. Quoted by John Glasser, in 'Conscience and Superego: A Key Distinction', *Theological Studies*, no. 32, 1971.

68. Quoted by R. Gross in *Psychology: the Science of Mind and Behaviour*, Hodder and Stoughton, London, 1992, p. 808.

69. Albert Gorres writes, 'When the superego is integrated into a mature conscience ... it relieves an individual from having constantly to decide in all these situations which are already legitimately decided by custom, taste, and convention 'what one should do' and 'what one should not do.''*Methode und Erfahrung der Psychoanalyse*, Munich, 1965, p. 169.

70. *Man Becoming*, NY, 1970, p. 223.

71. c.f. P Collins, *Intimacy and the Hungers of the Heart*, Columba, Dublin, 1991, pp.196-201.

72. Shafer, Hazan & Bradshaw, 'Love as Attachment' in *The Psychology of Love*, Yale, New Haven, 1988, p 80.

73. *Beyond Fear*, Fontana, London, 1987, p. 383. The neurotic fear of annihilation mentioned by Rowe is rooted in the ontological fear of annihilation mentioned by Tolstoy and Thérèse of Lisieux in chapter four.

74. *Treasures in Earthen Vessels: The Vows*, St Paul Publications, Slough, 1984, p. 50.

75. Op. cit. p. 181.

76. J Glaser, *Conscience and the Superego: a Key Distinction*, op. cit. p. 44.

77. Quoted by T Insel, in 'Phobias: Fear out of Control', *1986 Yearbook of*

Science and the Future, Encyclopedia Britannica, Inc., Chicago, p.182.

78. N Malleston, quoted in 'Phobic States, Treatment of,' by Isaac Marks in *Encyclopaedic Handbook of Medical Psychology* (ed. S Krauss) Butterworth, London, 1976, p. 390.

79. *c.f.* Isaac Marks, *Living With Fear*, Mc Graw-Hill, NY, 1980, 210-211; 213-214.

80. 'The Treatment of the Phobic and the Obsessive Compulsive Patient Using Paradoxical Intention,' in *Psychotherapy and Existentialism*, Penguin, London, 1973, pp. 171-185.

81. *c.f.* P Collins, 'Overcoming Stress' in *Growing in Health and Grace*, Campus, Galway, 1991, pp. 44-72.

82. *c.f.* Paul Hinnebusch, 'The Festal Shout,' Pt. 1 of *Praise a Way of Life*, Word of Life, Ann Arbor, 1977. pp. 11-55.

83. *The Psalms are our Prayers*, The Liturgical Press, Collegeville, Minnesota, 1964, p. 56.

84. *Praise a Way of Life*, op. cit. p. 230-237.

85. For a fascinating discussion of this subject see, E Ensley, *Sounds of Wonder*, Paulist Press, NY, 1977

PART 3: FAITH AND DELIVERANCE FROM EVIL

1. Quoted by R Mc Brien in *Catholicism*, Winston Press, Minneapolis, 1981, p. 14.

2. St Thomas Aquinas has pointed out that Satan cannot compel a person to sin. Human sin can only be committed with willing consent. Satan can tempt, try, test – he can never compel, and if he did compel the result would not be the sin of the one compelled. For more on this point see Victor White's *God and the Unconscious*, Fontana, London, 1960, pp. 197-1198.

3. *c.f.* K Rahner & H Vorgrimler, 'Possession' in *Theological Dictionary*, Herder & Herder, N.Y. 1965, p.365.

4. *Eternal Life*, Fount, London, 1985, p. 167.

5. H A Kelly, *The Devil, Demonology and Witchcraft*, N.Y. Doubleday, 1974.

6. P Collins, 'Exorcism and the Falling Phenomenon' in *Maturing in the Spirit*, Columba, Dublin, 1991, pp. 141-157.

7. 'Possessed by a Personal Devil?' *The Furrow*, June 1974, pp. 334-335.

8. In a simple exorcism a lay person or cleric prays that another person will be freed from the evil that oppresses one aspects of his or her life. In a solemn exorcism an officially appointed exorcist prays that another person will be freed from the evil that possesses his or her entire personality.

9. Paul VI, June 29, 1972.

10. General Audience Nov. 1973.

11. *Psychology as Religion: The Cult of Self-Worship*, Erdmans, Grand Rapids, 1980, pp. 38-50.

12. *Will and Spirit: A Contemplative Psychology*, Harper & Row, N.Y. 1982, pp. 10-11.

13. *Christian Faith and Demonology*, Vat. Collection II, Dominican Publications, Dublin, 1982, pp. 456-459.

14. *Eternal Life*, op. cit. p. 166.

15. *New Testament Theology*, SCM, London, 1981, p. 93.

16. *Christ: The Christian Experience in the Modern World*, SCM, London, 1980, p. 508.

17. *The Devil, Demonology, and Witchcraft*, op. cit. p. 23.

18. M Scanlon & R Cirner, *Deliverance from Evil Spirits*, Servant Publications, Ann Arbor, 1980, p.21.

19. *The New Jerome Biblical Commentary*, N.J. Prentice Hall, 1990, [78:20] p. 1321.

20. N.Y. 1960.

21. *God and the Unconscious*, op cit, pp. 188-203, and *Discernment: A Study in Ecstasy and Evil*, Paulist Press, N.Y. 1978, p. 64.

22. James Dunn, *Jesus and the Spirit*, SCM, London, 1975, p. 44.

23. *The Autobiography of Ignatius Loyola*, Harper Torchbooks, N.Y. 1974, p. 40.

24. Rahner & Vorgrimler, 'Devils and Demons,' *Theological Dictionary*, N.Y. 1965, p. 126-127.

25. 'Progress and Decline,' DLT, London, 1972, pp. 52-55.

26. Op. cit. p. 55.

27. Ed. Fogarty, Ryan & Lee, Dominican Publications, Dublin, 1984, p. 127.

28. *A Commentary on the Rules for Discernment of Spirits*, The Institute of Jesuit Resources, St. Louis, 1982, p. 262. (We have already noted that H Kung does not believe in the existence of a personal devil. Perhaps Toner doesn't think him a reputable theologian, in view of the fact that the Vatican has withdrawn his licence to teach Catholic theology.)

29. *Angels and Demons: The Teaching of IV Latern*, Theological Studies, XLII, No. 1, March 1981.

30. *Angels and Demons: the Teaching of IV Latern*, op. cit. p. 45.

31. *The Devil, Demonology & Witchcraft*, op. cit. p. 132 When I say that Kelly ignored Qual's conclusions, I do not mean it in a literal sense. I am aware that his book appeared before the latter's article on Latern IV was published.

32. 'Angels' in *Encyclopedia of Theology: A Concise Sacramentum Mundi*, Ed. K Rahner, Burns & Oates, London, 1975, p.9.

33. The assertion that evil is merely the lack of a good that should be there, but also an effective agent, a living perverted and perverting spiritual being, seems to modify the traditional notion of evil as the *privatio*

boni. Carl Jung would have approved. He once observed that the concentration camps of Nazi Germany could hardly be described as an accidental absence of perfection!

34. 'Deliver us from Evil,' L'Obsservatore Romano, Nov. 23, 1972

35. *Vatican Collection II*, op. cit. pp. 475-476

36. 'Deliver us from Evil' op. cit.

37. *Vatican Collection II*, op. cit. p. 478

38. c.f. P. Collins, *Intimacy and the Hungers of the Heart*, Columba, Dublin, 1991, pp. 66-68

39. *c.f.* J Aumann, *Spiritual Theology*, Sheed & Ward, London, 1982, pp. 402-404; 412, and K Leech, *Soul Friend*, Sheldon Press, London, 1977, p. 129-130

40. *Spiritual Theology*, op. cit. p. 407

41. *The Essence of Christianity*, p. iii

42. Quoted by H Kung in *Freud and the Problem of God*, Yale, New Haven, 1979, p. 75

43. 3rd. edition - revised, Washington: American Psychiatric Association, 1987

44. N Fodor, *Freud, Jung and Occultism*, p. 16

45. In Totemism a group or clan regards itself as being related to an animal, a plant or a natural phenomenon. It protects them.

46. *Leonardo Da Vinci and a Memory of his Childhood*, in SE 11, p. 123

47. *Does God Exist?*, Fount, London, 1978, p. 312

48. *Intimacy and the Hungers of the Heart*, op. cit., chap. 2

49. *Collected Works*, 12, par. 444

50. *Maturing in the Spirit*, op. cit., chap. 5

51. From 'The Psychology of Transference,' in *The Basic Writings of C G Jung*, Random House, N.Y. 1959, p. 420.

52. *Basic Writings*, op. cit. p. 420.

53. *Basic Writings*, op. cit. p. 420.

54. Jung wrote, 'There is no difference in principle between a fragmentary personality and a complex ... complexes are splinter psyches.' (*CW* 8, par. 202) 'Complexes behave like independent beings.' (*CW* 8, par. 253)

55. *Summa Theologiae: A concise Translation*, ed. T Mc Dermott, Methuen, p. 91

56. C G Jung, *Letters 2*, Princeton University Press, N.J. 1975, p. 61

57. *Freud, Jung and Occultism*, op. cit. p. 268

58. C G Jung, *Letters*, 2:1951-61, ed Adler & Jaffe, Princeton University Press, N.J. 1975, p. 624

59. *Civilization in Transition*, Pantheon Books, N.Y. 1964, p. 212

60. *Evil: The Shadow Side of Reality*, Crossroads, N.Y. 1981, chap. 5

61. In his many books Morton Kelsey has drawn attention to this important aspect of Jung's thinking and shown in experiential terms how the

realm of the supernatural, including evil spirits, impinges upon the psyche, e.g. *Discernment: A Study in Ecstasy and Evil*, op. cit esp. chaps. 3,4,&5

62. 'Psychology and Religion', in *Collected Works* Vol. 11. p. 335

63. May's use of the word 'daimonic' is confusing. In a footnote in *Love and Will* p. 123 he says, 'The word can be spelled 'demonic' or 'daemonic' or 'daimonic' (the derivative from the ancient Greek word 'diamon'). Since this last is the origin of the concept, and since the term is unambiguous in its including the positive as well as the negative, the divine as well as the diabolical, I use the Greek term.' I intend to retain May's term which he uses in its Greek sense to refer to purely psychological states, in order to distinguish it from its biblical counterpart, 'demonic' which refers to the state of being influenced by an unclean or evil spirit.

64. Fontana, London, 1972, p. 123

65. Quoted by H Egan in *Christian Mysticism: the Future of a Tradition*, Pueblo, N.Y. 1984, p. 351

66. *God and the Unconscious*, op. cit. p. 199. It is interesting to note that Jung and St Thomas had similar notions about the link between the world of matter, spirits, good and bad, and the human psyche. It is important in so far as it helps to explain how the devil can influence the activity of the mind. The former believed that the word of matter was linked to consciousness via each person's participation in the collective unconscious which could express itself in and through psychic archetypes e.g. the shadow and its complexes as it expresses itself in the form of fantasies, images, myths, symbols, feelings etc. Writing about the views of the latter, White writes, 'St Thomas has no doubt at all about what we should now call the physical basis of the human mind, and in particular of the spontaneous products of what we would now call undirected mentation or free phantasy ... Just as our ability to modify matter is limited by the potentialities and recourses of the matter at our disposal, so will be that of angels and demons. Satan (we may suppose) will exploit the psycho-spiritual make-up of those he favours with his attentions: the sanguine man will tend to mania, the melancholic to depression – the former will be more amenable to temptations to presumption, the latter to temptations to despair. But only when there is surrender of the will to these predetermined conditions can there be any question of sin: only then can Satan be said to have triumphed.' op. cit pp. 198-199. While it is true that sin is the greatest moral evil, we have seen that complexes can apparently lead to involuntary 'sin' in a compulsive way that bypasses the executive functions of the responsible ego.

67. *The Ghost in the Machine*, Pan, London, 1967, p. 269.

66. *Escape from Evil*, The Free Press, N.Y. 1976, pp. 92-95.

69. Quoted in *Time*, June 25, 1979, p. 33

70. *Discernment: A Study in Ecstasy and Evil*, op. cit. p.62

71. For more on this see, Michael Scanlon's *The Power in Penance: Confession and the Holy Spirit*, Ave Maria Press, Notre Dame, 1972, esp. pp. 52-53

72. *Deliverance from Evil Spirits*, op. cit. and *The Power in Penance*, op. cit.

73. *Irish Theological Quarterly*, Vol. XLI No. 4, Oct. 1974

74. 'Demonic Involvement in Human Life and Illness,' *Journal of Psychology and Theology* 5 (1977) p. 100

75. *People of the Lie: The Hope for Healing Human Evil*, Simon & Schuster, N.Y. 1983, p.182

76. BBC Radio 3, 1975

77. General audience, Nov. 15, 1972, Quoted in *Deliverance Prayer*, Ed. M Linn & D Linn, Paulist Press, N.Y. 1981, p. 10

78. *Jesus Christ and Mythology*, 1958, p. 15

79. Quoted by A Greeley in *The Jesus Myth*, Search Press, London, 1972, p. 11

80. *c.f.* C B Ruffin, *Padre Pio: The True Story*, Our Sunday Visitor Inc., Huntington, 1982, pp. 93-94. The Curé of Ars had similar experiences. See, 'The Devil Comes in Person,' in H Gehon, *Secrets of the Saints*, Sheed & Ward, London, 1973, pp. 90-111

81. Pub. Mentor, N.Y. 1977, esp. chap. 5. See also, Alice Miller, *For Your Own Good*, Farrar, Strauss & Giroux, N.Y. 1980, pp. 142-195

82. *Renewal and the Powers of Darkness*, DLT, London, 1983, pp. 31-32

83. *Renewal and the Powers of Darkness*, DLT London, 1983,pp. 31-32

84. 'This World Desperately Needs Theologians' *The Catholic Mind*, March 1981, p. 36

85. *Intimacy and the Hungers of the Heart*, op. cit. chaps 2 to 5

86. 'The Pain of Self-Discovery,' in *Intimacy and the Hungers of the Heart*, op. cit., chap. 4

87. *The Call to Conversion*, Lion, Tring, 1986, p. 5

88. *Early Christian Writings: The Apostolic Fathers*, Penguin Books, London, 1968, p. 228

89. *c.f. Maturing in the Spirit*, op. cit. pp. 142-144

90. *c.f.* 'Intercessory Prayer,' *Maturing in the Spirit*, op. cit. pp. 112-125

91. Surely there is a lot of truth in G May's statement, 'From the standpoint of purely intellectual thought, it makes a great difference whether evil forces are considered to be 'symbolic' or 'real.' But in the course of contemplative practice – and for that mater in any other setting in which such forces are experienced directly – the question becomes moot. If one finds oneself perceiving and reacting to evil forces, they must be dealt with.' 'Encounter with Evil' in *Will and Spirit*, op. cit. p. 272

PART 4: FAITH AND EUCHARISTIC HEALING

1. *Decree on the Ministry and Life of Priests,* No. 5
2. G. S. Sloyan, *Jesus in Focus: A Life in its Setting,* XXIII Publications, Mystic, Con. 1983, p. 36. 'The word *hasid* in Hebrew is related to the noun *hesed* which is often translated "loving kindness." The *hasidim* were charismatic holy men, who were noted for their holiness and their deeds of power. J. P. Meir, 'Jesus' in *The New Jerome Biblical Commentary,* Prentice Hall, N.J. 1990, 78:43, p. 1325. 'Vermes (Jesus the Jew 58-85) points out that alongside the professional Scribes and pious Pharisees there existed holy men – in some cases, from Galilee – famous for miracles or exorcisms. They were the products of popular folk religion rather than academic theology.'
2. Sloyan, op. cit. p. 37
3. *Healing & Christianity: In Ancient Thought and Modern Times,* SCM, London, 1973, p. 67
4. *The Pope in Ireland: Addresses and Homilies,* Veritas, Dublin 1979, p. 57
5. George Montague, *Riding the Wind,* Word of Life, Ann Arbor, 1977, p. 56-57
6. Kathryn Kuhlman, *I Believe in Miracles,* Lakeland, London, 1972, p.198
7. *Matthew: New Testament Message* 3, Veritas, Dublin, 1984, pp. 60-61
8. P Collins, *Maturing in the Spirit,* Dublin, Columba, 1991, pp. 144-149
9. *The Pope in Ireland: Addresses and Homilies,* pp77-78
10. 'Anxiety' op. cit. Harper Torchbooks, N.Y. 1966, Part 4, chap. 11, p. 207
11. Op. cit., p. 207
12. Leon-Dufour, *Dictionary of the New Testament,* Harper & Row, N.Y. 1980, p. 316
13. Charlesworth & Nathan, *Stress Management,* Ballentine, N.Y. 1985, p. v10
14. H Benson, *Beyond the Relaxation Response: How to Harness the Healing Power of your Personal Beliefs,* Fount, London, 1985, p. 76
15. Post Communion prayer, Monday of the first week of Lent.
16. *Mystagogical Catecheses,* V, 21-22, quoted by L Deiss in *It's the Lord's Supper: The Eucharist of Christians,* Collins, Flame, London, 1986, p. 153
17. *c.f.* F Mc Nutt, *The Power to Heal,* Ave Maria Press, Notre Dame, 1977, pp. 247-249
18. J Mc Manus, *The Healing Power of the Sacraments,* Ave Maria Press, 1984, pp. 101-105
19. *Apostolic Tradition of Hippolytus* I.5.
20. Quoted by M Kelsey, *Healing and Christianity,* op. cit., p. 181.
21. *The Rite of Anointing of the Sick.*
22. St Augustine has written, 'He who suffered for us entrusted to us the

sacrament of his own Body and Blood; into this he also makes us. We are become his Body and are that which we receive through his mercy. *Sermon* 109. Interestingly, Jung wrote, 'The mixing of water and wine in the Roman Rite would accordingly signify that divinity is mingled with humanity as indivisibly as the wine with the water.' 'Transformation Symbolism and the Mass' in *Psychology and Religion: West and East*, RKP, London.

23. 'On the Mystery and Worship of the Eucharist,' Flannery (ed.) *Vatican Collection Vol. 2*, par. 7. p. 72

24. For more on this see B. J Groeschel, *Spiritual Passages: The Psychology of Spiritual Development*, Crossroads, N.Y. 1986, esp. Part II, 'A Psychological Understanding of the Three Ways.'

24. *c.f.* J Welch, *Spiritual Pilgrims: Carl Jung & Teresa of Avila*, Paulist Press, N.Y. 1982

25. *Transpersonal Development: The Dimension beyond Psychosynthesis*, Crucible, London, 1991, esp. pp. 155-169

26. *Will and Spirit*, Harper & Row, N.Y. 1987

27. Roberto Assagioli described the link between the heating of the elements and the dynamics of psycho-spiritual transformation, 'Substances subjected to this process pass through three transformations: in the first stage they become black – this is referred to as the decomposition stage and relates to the stage of purging or purification spoken of by the mystics – then in the second stage they become white, being transformed into silver – this refers to the enlightenment of the soul. Finally, at the third stage, which is the highest, they become red, and are transformed into gold, the spiritual gold – this marks completion of the Magnum Opus and corresponds to the glorious state of unity referred to by the mystics.' 'Transmutation and Sublimation of Emotional and Sexual Energies' in *Transpersonal Development*, op cit p. 209

28. 'Transformation Symbolism in the Mass' in *Psychology and Religion: West and East*, op. cit pp. ??

29. For more on this see P. Collins, 'The Pain of Self Discovery,' in *Intimacy and the Hungers of the Heart*, Columba, Dublin, 1991, pp 58-74

30. Quoted by P Coste in *The Life and Works of St Vincent de Paul*, Vol 1, New City Press, N.Y. p. 353

31. Address to the Eucumenical Meeting Dublin, Sept 29, 1979, in *The Pope in Ireland: Addresses and Homilies*, Veritas, Dublin, 1979, p. 35

32. In a well researched chapter entitled, 'Modern Christianity and Healing,' M Kelsey, has outlined the many reasons why the Church neglected its healing ministry, e.g. the devastating effects of the Barbarian invasions on Christian Europe, the ascendency of Aristotelian rationalism which had little room for healing, the emphasis on spiritual as opposed to physical or mental healing in the sacrament of 'extreme

unction,' and because popular forms of healing were often superstitious in nature. *Healing and Christianity*, SCM, London, 1973, pp 200-242

33. *The Constitution on the Church*, par. 12

34. Pope John Paul II, *The Vocation and Mission of the Lay Faithful in the Church and the World*, par. 20

35. c.f. p. 23-24 section 1, above, and P Collins, 'Baptism in the Spirit' in *Maturing in the Spirit*, Columba, Dublin, 1991, pp. 26- 40

36. c.f. Morton Kelsey, *Healing and Christianity*, SCM. Press, London, 1973, pp. 179-182

37. Translated by Philip Weller, Bruce, Milwaukee, 1964. *c.f.* J Mc Manus, *The Healing Power of the Sacraments*, Ave Maria Pres, Notre Dame, 1984, pp 101-105 and F McNutt, *The Power to Heal*, Ave Maria Press, 1977, pp 247- 254. Mc Nutt includes a blessing for holy water which can also be used for healing purposes.

38. When he was in Ireland in 1979, Pope John Paul II said, 'Our full participation in the Eucharist is the real source of the Christian spirit that we wish to see in our personal lives and in all aspects of society. Whether we serve in politics, in the economic, cultural, social, or scientific fields – no matter what our occupation is – the Eucharist is a challenge to our daily lives ... There must always be consistency between what we believe and what we do ... Each Eucharist is a call to be ... generous in our deeds, concerned, respectful of the dignity and rights of all persons whatever their rank or income.' Homily during Mass at the Phoenix Park, Dublin, 29th. Sept. in *The Pope in Ireland: Addresses and Homilies*, Veritas, Dublin, 1979, p.11

39. Quoted in 'Karl Pribram's Changing Reality' in The *Holographic Paradigm and Other Paradoxes*, (Ed.) Ken Wilber, Shambhala Publications Inc. Boulder, 1982, p. 25

40. He explored this theme in some of his writings such as, 'The Mass on the World' and 'Christ in the World of Matter: Three stories in the Style of Benson' in *Hymn of the Universe*, Collins, London, 1965. He wrote, 'As our humanity assimilates the material world, and as the Host assimilates our humanity, the eucharistic transformation goes beyond and completes the transubstantiation of the bread on the altar. Step by step it irresistibly invades the universe. It is the fire that sweeps over the heath; the stroke that vibrates through the bronze. In a secondary and generalised sense, but in a true sense, the sacramental species are formed by the totality of the world, and the duration of creation is the time needed for its consecration. In Christ we live and move and have our being.' *Le Milieu Divin*, Fontana, London, 1965. pp. 125-126.

41. c.f. Jim Mc Manus, *The Healing Power of the Sacraments*, Redemptorist Publications/Ave Maria Press, Notre Dame, 1984, chap. 6. Michael Scan-

lon, *And Their Eyes Were Opened*, Servant Publications, Ann Arbor.
42. *New Covenant*, Nov 1979
43. 'Priests and Scholars: 2 A Word of Warning,' *Kings, Lords, & Commons*, Gill & Macmillan, Dublin, 1970, p. 16

Index